INDUSTRIAL RELATIONS MONOGRAPH NO. 30

# NEW DIMENSIONS IN ORGANIZATION

# PREFACE

Some years ago, when behavioral science became a topic of interest in business circles, management felt the need for a closer contact with the research being done in the field, and IRC was asked to try to bridge the gap. In 1962, therefore, we scheduled a symposium at which we invited six university men to present papers on the results of their research in behavioral science and to suggest how behavioral science might apply to the business world.

After this symposium, however, we found we had begun a dialogue of which only one side had been heard. How had management applied behavioral science in industry, and how did the theories hold up away from the controlled experimental situation? To answer these questions, we scheduled a second symposium on behavioral science, inviting members of management to speak.

Thus the IRC Symposium on Advanced Research in Industrial Relations was established as an annual event, and until 1968 we continued the pattern of discussing one topic at two succeeding meetings, inviting academic speakers the first year and representatives of management the next year. University scholars invited to the 1966 symposium discussed the results of their research into the personality and role relationships within organizational units; the following year management representatives were asked to discuss the application of organization theory in day-to-day business situations, with emphasis on new methods and how they have worked or not worked. Papers from both groups are brought together in this book, and we at IRC hope that this diversity of viewpoints will give our readers an overall view of the new theories and methods of organization and will be of help to management in solving organizational problems.

We extend our thanks to all who participated in the symposia on organization theory, including those whose contributions to the discussions could not be reflected in this book, which, of course, is not a complete record of the meetings. We especially thank Professor William Starbuck of Cornell University and Mr. Francis P. McKiernan of American Can Company for stimulating oral presentations which are not recorded here. Thanks are also due to the speakers who assisted in the preparation of this book by adapting their papers for publication in this form.

It should further be noted that the paper by Dr. Frederick Lippert is of later date than the meeting at which he spoke, since Dr. Lippert was kind enough to update his contribution to include the results of later research.

Richard A. Beaumont
President
Industrial Relations Counselors, Inc.

January, 1970.

Preface

RICHARD A. BEAUMONT **11** *Introduction*

ALLEN H. BARTON **21** *The Organization as a Social Entity*

ALVIN F. ZANDER **37** *The Desire for Group Achievement*

ABRAHAM ZALEZNIK **55** *External and Internal Role Conflict*

ROBERT L. KAHN **70** *The Open System and Role Conflict*

HERBERT A. SHEPARD **89** *Integrating the Individual with the Organization*

HARVEY SHERMAN **99** *A Pragmatic Approach to Organization*

J. H. McPHERSON **111** *The Small Group, the Organization, and the Creativity Domain*

FRANK J. JASINSKI **121** *Dealing with Group Conflict— A Problem-Centered Approach*

JAMES E. RICHARD **137** *Innovation and Experimentation in a Rapidly Growing Organization*

FREDERICK G. LIPPERT **149** *Authoritarianism and Role Pressure in Participative Leadership*

## RICHARD A. BEAUMONT

*President, Industrial Relations Counselors, Inc.,* Mr. Beaumont has long been active in research on management organization and industrial relations. He joined the organization in 1958 and in 1961 was made director of research. He became president in 1964. From January, 1966, to August, 1967, Mr. Beaumont was on leave, serving as Deputy Under Secretary of the Navy. He has served as a consultant to major corporations in this country and abroad, to the Department of the Navy, and to state and local governments, and is also president of a New York management consulting firm, Organization Resources Counselors, Inc.

# INTRODUCTION

Industrial Relations Counselors has in its charter the mission "to advance the knowledge and practice of human relationships in commerce, industry, education and government." It is within this framework that we are concerned with organization theory and practice. Organizations have needs—expressed, for instance, in the establishment of goals and objectives; people too have needs. We have come to realize that unless the ways to satisfy these needs can be brought into some degree of congruency, organizations lose their effectiveness. The symposium papers presented here deal with a variety of theories and programs that have been developed in the effort to overcome such problems.

*Richard Beaumont*

## Organization Theory: The Major Schools

Organization theory marries the systematic approaches required in studying organizations to the more qualitative approaches needed in studying human relations factors, those that derive from the people who make up an organization, who in themselves are not quite so systematic. Looking back on organization theory through the years, we might say that there have been four major schools.

The classical school emphasized structure, hierarchy, and the application of military organizational principles to the industrial scene. It attempted to distinguish between line and staff, and was concerned with such ideas as span of control and levels within an organization. Application of the classical theory, however, created structures that might look good but that didn't always achieve the objectives for which they were established. As a consequence, various mechanistic approaches were developed to cope with the problems the classical school had not solved.

This second school might be termed the mechanistic school. Its influence was greatest in the United States in the 1920's. It called, for example, for the application of job evaluations, based on job descriptions. This was an attempt to establish very clear, functional statements of the job tasks of each and every organizational unit. The idea was that if, within the organization structure, we could discover and remedy what was wrong with relationships in terms of duties and responsibilities, we could get the organization to function as planned.

A third school, concurrent with the mechanistic approach, was the scientific management group. This school was looking for efficiency—in essence, the most efficient means of accomplishing the job within a set of specifications. Their methods involved work simplification, work measurement, time and motion study, and the establishment of incentive techniques for particular pieces of output. The idea here was to establish a very careful control of each small element of the organization and to build systematically from the basic work element.

The fourth major group might be called the psychological or human relations school; it was concerned with the dynamics of people within the organization. This school examined goals and goal accomplishment, groups and group behavior, and the importance of job satisfaction.

I will go further and say that there is perhaps a fifth school beginning to emerge today, although its theories certainly haven't been codified into a single approach toward organization. This group attempts to examine and evaluate (and perhaps shape and mold) leadership, realizing that leadership has a very strong influence on what happens within an organization. It examines how the decision-making process shapes the organizational map; it also takes into account small-group behavior and its influence, the social structure of the organization, etc.

As we at IRC have thought about these great schools of organization theory and their contributions, we have sometimes been disquieted. Despite the theory, despite the analysis, we have seen organizations that seem badly set out on a chart work effectively and efficiently, provide satisfactions to the people involved, and accomplish the objectives of the organization. On the other hand, we have seen marvelous structures, with great amounts of staff time applied to the scrutiny and constant refurbishment of the organization, that seem to lack the capability or the spark to achieve their objectives.

Hundreds of times I have heard from sage people with years of experience in this field that the best structured organization might never work but the worst structured organization can be made to work if it has the right people in it. Starting with that observation, I have been reflecting on my recent experience as part of the Department of Defense and have been trying to deduce what made it work, in the hope that some answers to major organizational problems might be found in that structure.

**The Team Approach**

There are four and a half million people in the Department of Defense, yet it is really run by the civilian Secretariat, which consists of the Secretary and about 45 people. What are some of the characteristics of the Department? It has a high esprit de corps. The 45 people are a team; they have a clear idea of the mission they are to accomplish, although each might define the mission somewhat differently because of his particular background and expertise. This team is highly dedicated, highly motivated. It wants to achieve what it is there to accomplish and it wants to do so in the most efficient way possible. Therefore, under Secretary McNamara, it took as one of its key principles the idea of cost effectiveness. Unfortunately, at this point the concept of cost effectiveness extends only to things, not people.

The people in the civilian Secretariat are primarily engaged in long-term planning. They are intimately involved in appraising what has been done and hold subordinates highly accountable for it. When this central group deviates from the long-term planning function, it is to engage in solving a particular problem that for some reason or other the organization itself cannot solve. Thus they are not normally involved in current day-to-day business or with short-term plans that might be related to a budget period. Finally, the team is involved in policy formulation. In each of these four areas — planning, appraisal, problem solving, and policy making—there is a growing tendency to centralize each process within this group of 45 people.

I find that in our own organization at IRC we also have a concept of team. And industry, too, seems to be moving toward the team approach.

As one looks at the industrial scene, he is first struck by the growth of large-scale endeavors, particularly where there are highly automated operations and large investments in warehousing, inventory control systems, computer and data processing systems, and the like. Growth is not simply a phenomenon that takes place with increased economic activity but rather arises as a result of the economies of scale so essential in modern-day enterprise, scale which requires a greater application of capital resources to the running of the business and, in turn, an adequate return on investment. But along with the growth among the giants of industry, we also seem to have a proliferation of small groups, either as independent operations or as groups within the major corporate structure.

*Richard Beaumont*

I know many of you in this audience represent companies that have set up very specialized functional groups to deal with a particular product or service. Typically, these products or services are esoteric, unusual, or new in terms of your normal business; thus they require the establishment of groups that can bring new expertise to the project areas. The need may be for a combination of scientific people, managerial people, and other personnel who normally would not be found in a specific corporate department. Many companies therefore create small, quasi-independent establishments or units. Without such units it is highly unlikely that product success or market penetration will be achieved. In the government, this method of creating new structure is called project management; in business, the groups are called special task forces, special planning groups, special product groups, special marketing establishments, etc.

Small, independent organizations—and there have been many of them, particularly in the computer field, in software and in market services — have been created for many of the same reasons. For example, Scientific Data Systems is big now, but it started from a four-man group — a mathematical genius, an accountant, a marketing genius who helped sell the idea, and a production specialist.

**The Impact of Growth**

What I am suggesting is that as organizations get bigger they need smaller units to accomplish work within the organization itself, units with specific, clearly defined goals. And as these groups evolve and emerge, it seems to me that fundamental changes are taking place in our view of how an organization achieves its goals and, in turn, in organization theory.

Still other phenomena are occuring as a result of the increasing size and complexity of organizations. One is that the problems that organizations deal with tend to have less precise answers.

There is no simple answer to whether your company should market a product under the name X, Y, or Z, or to whether it should market the product in geographic area A, B, or C, or to what its size or shape should be. Many people have good ideas on what should be done with a given product in a given product market. The great difficulty is in choosing among the possible good solutions. Also, as our organizations and our problems become larger, more and more people have a say in the final answer, so that the final answer is not the logical, precise one that we would hope an organization should produce, but is rather a combination of viewpoints and ideas.

A second observation I would like to make in this connection is that as organizations become larger and their problems become more complex, the organization itself is in less of a position to make a decision; the customer, or the government, or someone else has a degree of influence on the organization's decision-making process. Certainly those of you in the personnel field can see this happening today in your employment practices. What you are doing in the equal employment field now is not a result of your own decision but of collective decisions made for you, with you, and by you as a result of what has taken place in the community at large. You as a supplier on a government contract are not making your own decisions with respect to the product to be produced. As a supplier of electrical generating equipment to public utility companies, you are not making your own decisions about the shape, size, or characteristics of that equipment. Decision-making for a corporation is often not confined to those within the organization.

A third point is that the larger the organization, the more difficulty it has in responding to change, because the larger you are the more you are geared to a systematic way of doing things. Therefore size itself is an impediment to making rapid decisions involving fundamental change.

**The Dynamics of Change**

While our organizations are changing, the people within the organizations are changing also. We all know how much better educated the group that we deal with today is. The recent college graduate has different ideas of what he would like to achieve in his work career than perhaps you or his parents did; he has higher degrees of aspiration and his aspiration seems to increase geometrically with his educational attainment. We all know that the new graduates seem to need intellectual stimulation and job satisfaction of a more abstract nature, than did the worker of 20, 30, or 40 years ago who simply wanted to be comfortable, satisfied, and rewarded properly through his work. Today there is also greater mobility of people — perhaps as a result of a lower degree of identification with the company.

How do we relate these factors to what is taking place on the industrial and governmental scene? This, it seems to me, is one of the major challenges we have in the field of organization planning, management development, and human relations in industry. Organizations change, their needs change, and people in the organizations change, and these elements are not always changing at the same rate at any given point in time. Therefore, bringing the needs of the organization into congruency with its people's needs and interests is not a simple process; it requires the development of a multivariant system to achieve the goals of the organization. There has never been a compensation scheme, a human relations program, a program of sensitivity training — in fact, no one technique, whether developed by the classicists or mechanists or scientific management or human relations people — that solved all the fundamental organizational problems with which we deal.

Therefore, I would like to suggest that our approach to the theories and programs outlined in the following papers should be discriminating, should go beyond the particularized approach to see how that approach, if it works, fits a given organization at a given point in time. How does it relate to the other approaches and concepts which are needed to make the organization work, and to the people who are there and who must make it work?

**ALLEN H. BARTON**

*Director of the Bureau of Applied Social Research and Associate Professor of Sociology, Columbia University.* A member of the faculty of Columbia University since 1957, Professor Barton became director of the Bureau of Applied Social Research in 1962. He has also served as a lecturer in sociology at the University of Oslo (1948-1949) and as assistant professor of sociology at the School of Law, University of Chicago (1954-1957).

20

# THE ORGANIZATION AS A SOCIAL ENTITY

Social scientists generally agree that a formal organization is a social system in which a set of people engage in activities coordinated by relatively consistent expectations about one another and relatively accurate flow of information, and these activities achieve sufficient results to maintain equilibrium or possibly to increase the size, knowledge, or resources of the organization.

What is "formal" about such an organization, as compared with other social systems like families, communities, friendship groups, or interest groups, is that it has more clearly labeled jobs or offices (statuses); more explicit rules governing the behavior of people in

21

these statuses (role prescriptions); and more precise purposes (formal goals). In this way, a formal organization can coordinate a large and rapidly changing set of persons to achieve a relatively constant set of purposes. A family or friendship group, on the other hand, takes a long time to indoctrinate a member into the appropriate behavior and tends to shift its goals according to the people who belong to it.

Given the emphasis on the interdependency of the parts of an organization, it is natural that there is a great deal of interest in the relationship between the behavior of one group and that of another — for example, the foreman's style of leadership and workers' output or the amount of communication between departments to the degree of consensus between them.

There are numerous propositions about these relationships, some of which are grouped under the heading of "functional analysis" — for example, that the function of maintaining social distance between superiors and subordinates is to permit objective treatment of requests for resources and fair evaluation of output. Some theorists have tried to organize these propositions into axiomatic systems, mathematical models, or simulation models. Herbert Simon, Richard Cyert, James March, and others have worked out examples that are quite sophisticated mathematically and logically. If not Einsteinian, they look, at least, Newtonian — full of mathematical functions, coefficients, variables, and constants. If the Copernican revolution in organization theory was the realizaton by Mayo and his colleagues that organizations were not simply gangs of economic men, then the Newtonian revolution in organization theory should be a set of mathematical laws predicting how men will behave in the social system of the organization.

## Deficiencies in Organization Research

What I want to talk about today, however, is the gap between these sophisticated techniques of modeling and the quality of the data actually collected; and I want to indicate the kinds of research needed to fill the gap.

The fact is that we do not have accurate ways of measuring many of the variables that should go into such models, nor do we use research designs that would permit us to test the relationships between these variables when they are measured.

If you want a demonstration of this, just glance at the main inventory of organizational propositions, March and Simon's *Organizations*.[1] Much of the evidence for the relationships they discuss comes from qualitative, observational studies, which don't produce systematic statistical data, but verbal descriptions — Merton's general analysis of bureaucracy, Selznick's qualitative study of one government-owned enterprise, Gouldner's qualitative study of one industrial plant, Roethlisberger and Dickson's observations in the bank wiring room. Many variables that they discuss have never been measured — even by the low standards of social science research—but only subjectively reported.

It is true that there have also been many quantitative studies and that March and Simon cite results from them. However, the design of these studies is usually inadequate for studying the laws govern-

1. James G. March and Herbert A. Simon, *Organizations* (New York: Wiley, 1958).

ing social systems. Let us look at some of their typical deficiencies.

1. Most studies examine only one stratum within the system, usually the rank-and-file level, and analyze it without reference to what other people in that system are doing. The result is a one-sided view of role relationships. Even when a study does consider two or more status levels within the organization, more often than not it obtains no information on who is related to whom. In other words, we have samples of foremen and workers, but do not know which worker goes with which foreman.

2. Researchers use atomistic samples—every *nth* person—and consequently never question two people who interact with one another. Furthermore, the sample is rarely large enough to permit us even to characterize the group context of the respondent. A relational survey, which not only studies people in different positions but is designed to obtain information on their relationships, can produce a lot of data not obtainable from simple one-stratum or multistratum surveys.

3. On the few occasions when we do have samples of role partners, identified as such, and obtain information on their behavior, attitudes, or role expectations, the information is static. That is, we do not have information on the sequence of changes in relationships, which might permit us to demonstrate casual relationships. Consider all the studies that have correlated the foreman's style of leadership with workers' morale and output. Do any of these studies contain evidence as to which causes the other—i.e., does harsh behavior by the foreman lead to low output, or does low output by the workers lead to harsh behavior by the foreman?

There is one actual experiment, done by Morse and Reimer at Michigan, in which supervisor behavior was deliberately changed, and subsequent changes in worker output were observed.[2] This, as we all know, showed that close supervision results in greater output than does worker autonomy. However, the experiment was not carried on long enough, it has never been repeated, and the experimental design, in which foreman behavior was manipulated, could not test whether foreman behavior was also influenced by worker behavior.

4. When considering the characteristics of an organization as a whole, we have only the most primitive information about its basic features—for example, the relation of technology to management structure, as studied by Joan Woodward in 100 English firms,[3] and the relation of administration to production personnel, as studied by Haire in half a dozen organizations.[4] We lack large-sample studies that permit multivariate analysis of organizational characteristics.

**New Directions**

In the past few years, several groups of studies have risen above this primitivism of design. Let me mention a few of these.

**1. Studies that permit analysis of the effects of environment on persons in many organizational units.** "Contextual analysis" was developed by Paul Lazarsfeld in his study of the effect of McCarthyism on college professors in the social sciences.[5]

From the responses of professors at 156 institutions to questions about their attitudes and behavior, Lazarsfeld was able to compute

**2.** Nancy Morse and E. Reimer, "The Experimental Change of a Major Organizational Variable," *Journal of Abnormal and Social Psychology*, LII (1956), 120-129. **3.** Joan Woodward, *Management and Technology* (London: Her Majesty's Stationery Office, 1958). **4.** Mason Haire, "Biological Models and Empirical Histories of the Growth of Organizations," in *Modern Organization Theory*, ed. Mason Haire (New York: Wiley, 1959), pp. 272-306. **5.** Paul F. Lazarsfeld and Wagner Thielens, Jr., *The Academic Mind* (Glencoe, Illinois: The Free Press, 1958).

measures of "faculty climate"—that is, liberal, conservative, or mixed; apprehensive or secure. From reports on the behavior of the college administration and local politicians, and on "incidents" threatening academic freedom, he computed measures of the degree of attack to which the institution was subject and of the degree of "administrative protectiveness" for the academic freedom of the faculty. In this way, he could analyze how professors at different kinds of institutions were affected.

The same method was applied in a study of New York City law offices, directed by Jerome Carlin for the Bureau of Applied Social Research.[6] Carlin found that the ethical climate of the law office had a powerful influence on the behavior of lawyers when their individual ethical attitudes were held constant. The entire analysis presents a complicated picture of the social and religious factors that influence recruitment to firms of various sizes; the stratification of the bar and the nature of work of the various strata; the moral division of labor between large and small firms that exposes the individual or small-firm practitioner to severe pressures and easy opportunities for unethical conduct; and the role of both personal values and the law office climate in regulating ethical behavior.

Another Columbia study used samples of students from 99 campuses to examine college cheating.[7] Once again, the moral climate of the peer group and of the college as a whole, as well as their own internalized values, has an enormous effect on students. The percentage of students who have ever seriously cheated ranges from 8 percent to 80 percent; the increasing percentages correlate strongly with the size of the institution, its having a nonintellectual climate, the number of students per teacher, the lack of student-faculty contact, and lack of academic selectivity. There is also strong evidence that the student culture, under certain conditions, can be harnessed by an honor system to drastically reduce cheating. This demonstrates not only the power of the social context, but the ability of formal institutions to work with informal systems toward common goals.

Studies in industry seldom exploit the possibility of contextual analysis, although samples are often drawn in ways that would permit measuring contextual attributes of subunits.

**2. Studies that inquire into role expectations and behavior of both partners of a role relationship.** A pioneering project by Stogdill, Scott, and Jaynes at Ohio State studied 47 superiors and one or two subordinates of each superior in a naval research and development command.[8] The superiors were asked how frequently they did each of 45 types of behavior, such as "represent subordinates," "prepare charts," "consult subordinates," and "perform mathematical computations." They were also asked how frequently they thought they should do each. The subordinates were asked how frequently they did each thing, how frequently they should do it, how frequently their superior did it, and how frequently he should do it.

Although we do not have completely symmetrical data—superiors were not asked about subordinates—the results permitted the researchers to make some very interesting observations. Most superiors and subordinates said they were doing what they should be doing ($r=.70$), but there was a very low consensus between superiors and

**6.** Jerome E. Carlin, *Lawyers' Ethics* (New York: Russell Sage Foundation, 1966).
**7.** William Bowers, *Student Dishonesty and its Control in College* (New York: Bureau of Applied Social Research, 1964).
**8.** R. M. Stogdill, *et al., Leadership Role Expectations* (Columbus, Ohio: Bureau of Business Research, Monograph 86, 1958).

subordinates on what the superior should be doing (r=. 21). There was a very low correspondence between what the superior said he was doing and what the subordinate said the superior was doing (r=.16), and a low correspondence between any two subordinates on what the superior was doing.

Does this indicate that an organization can get along with a minimum of consensus, even between immediate role-partners, as to what each person should be doing? Or did the researchers simply ask the wrong questions?

Two years after the Ohio State study, Neal Gross and his colleagues came out with their brilliantly designed study *Explorations in Role Analysis* — a study of role expectations of school boards and school superintendents.[9] Here 137 questions were asked of 100 school superintendents and of an average of five school board members for each superintendent. Unfortunately, the only striking relationships found involved the local peculiarities of Massachusetts politics and the special role of Catholic-Protestant divisions on the school board, as they affected the superintendent.

Despite these studies, we have yet to see one that bears, for instance, on the question of what role elements we should sample to get some measure of the degree of role consensus in any role relationship; or how much consensus, and between which members of the organization, is necessary for the organization to function; or how much knowledge of role performance various role partners should have. The postulate of complete role consensus is dead, but exactly what theory has replaced it is unclear.

*Allen H. Barton*

The recent study by Kahn, Wolfe, Quinn, Snoek, and Rosenthal used a "snowball" design to measure attitudes and behaviors of about seven members of the role set—including superiors, subordinates, and peers—of each of 53 managers and foremen.[10] A number of highly interesting relationships were found between the degree of satisfaction of members of the role set and the performance and psychological state of the focal person. Unfortunately, the design was not exploited to obtain detailed information on role expectations within the role set, so that we lack information on situations where superiors, subordinates, and peers expect different behavior.

**3. Studies that examine reciprocal changes in behavior or attitudes over time.** Stanton and Schwartz, in their classic qualitative study of a mental hospital, came to the conclusion, after looking at records of six patients over 19 months, that patient disturbance was strongly related to covert staff disagreement about how the patient was to be handled.

Anthony Wallace and H. A. Rashkis tried to quantify these concepts by observing two small samples of patients over a number of weeks and obtaining measures of patient disturbance and staff dissensus on each patient's condition and treatment.[11] In one sample there was no relationship, but in the other, two interesting facts came to light. First, staff disagreement tended to be followed by patient disturbance and, patient disturbance tended to be followed by staff disagreement. If the relationships had been high enough we would have had a cycle of uncontrolled positive feedback—vicious for the disturbed patient who was the object of disagreement and

**9.** Neal Gross, et al., *Explorations in Role Analysis* (New York: Wiley, 1964).
**10.** R. L. Kahn, et al., Organizational Stress: Studies in *Role Conflict and Ambiguity* (New York: Wiley, 1964).
**11.** H. A. Rashkis and H. F. C. Wallace, "The Reciprocal Effect: How Patient Disturbance is Affected by Staff Attitudes," *American Medical Association Archives of General Psychiatry*, I (1959), 489-498.

Allen H. Barton

benign for the nondisturbed or agreed-upon patient. It is important to note that the relationship was not just from the behavior of the staff to that of the patients, but also the other way around.

When will we have a study of the reciprocal impact of the foreman and his work group? Or a study of the progressive changes that take place when a new employee, at any level, enters a firm or plant, which would be equally interesting?

Ten years ago, Dr. Bernard Levenson of the Bureau of Applied Social Research wrote a proposal for a study of problems of organizational promotion.[12] He was given neither money nor access to an organization, and consequently his plan remains a classic theoretical paper. Levenson starts by noting that the manager who rises is said to be characterized by the following personal traits: he delegates responsibility, keeps subordinates well informed, and creates high morale and productivity. Levenson suggests that the relationship actually may be the reverse—the manager, knowing that he may be promoted, tries to prepare for and hasten that day by getting his successor and people all along the line below him ready to move up. His subordinates see a chance to get ahead and they make a greater effort and delegate more in order to avoid being so essential in their current positions that management does not dare promote them. Conversely, the manager who knows he is not moving up has no incentive to train a potential successor, and his subordinates can hope to be promoted only out of his department or by catching the attention of superiors in other departments, thus bypassing the unpromotable boss.

30

This is all good, logical speculation. However, to test the relative stability and importance of personality traits as compared with situationally induced behavior, we need a study of superiors and subordinates in various departments during a period when some are in process of moving up and others are discovering that they are not.

**4. Evaluation studies that take the peer group into account.** A particularly interesting use of the relational panel design is an evaluation study of the effect of campaigns, either within organizations or within communities. It has long been known that many information campaigns fail, as pointed out in an article by Hyman and Sheatsley.[13] At the Bureau we are now reviewing evaluation studies of social action programs intended to prevent delinquency, mental illness, poverty, etc., and are finding that most of them fail too.

Yet, the design of these studies seldom tells us why the program failed. A plausible hypothesis is that most people are more strongly influenced by their interpersonal environment—friends, relatives, neighbors, and fellow workers—than by a mass media campaign or occasional, brief contact with social workers, psychiatrist, or educators. People who are poor, delinquent, or prejudiced belong to social groups that share these traits.

Exposure to convincing persuasion from outside their environment may fail to move people because they are "locked in" by the attitudes and expectations of their peers and immediate superiors. If we were to shift our sample from individuals to peer groups—or, where they did not form neat groups, took a "snowball sample" of the three or four people with whom the respondent spent the most time—we

12. Bernard Levenson, "Bureaucratic Succession," in *Complex Organization,* ed. Amitai Etzioni (New York: Holt, Rinehart and Winston,1961.
13. Herbert Hyman and Paul Sheatsley, "Some Reasons Why Information Campaigns Fail," *Public Opinion Quarterly,* II (1947), 412-423.

could then examine the attitudes of the peer group and the sanctions that might be exerted against change, and we might then understand why some people change and others do not. We might also find the opposite phenomenon. If one member of a peer group in an urban slum overcomes the cynicism and apathy of the group, gets job training, and moves into a good job, will this now feed back to the others, raise their aspirations, and produce a multiplier effect?

To my knowledge, evaluation studies — whether in industry or elsewhere — have not exploited relational panels in order to study these opposing processes.

**5. Studies that permit multivariate analysis of organizational characteristics within large samples of organizations.** Such a study is being carried out by Peter Blau at the University of Chicago.[14] He is studying a large number of public agencies that perform similar functions in order to obtain information on such variables as division of labor, professionalization, hierarchy, administrative apparatus, operating cost, and size of population served.

One of the outstanding findings of Blau's study is that these variables are not related in a simple, additive, linear way; instead there are strong interactional effects. For example, the effect of size on hierarchy depends upon how professionalized the agency is; its effect on cost depends upon a combination of division of labor and amount of administrative apparatus. Consequently, it appears that our propositions concerning the broad shape and form of organizations cannot be simple, two-variable statements, but rather must be multi-variate hypotheses, stating the conditions under which they are true.

*Allen H. Barton*

## Empirical Data and Model Building

The shortcomings of social science data, particularly in measurement procedures, prevent easy borrowing of physical science models. However, it should be possible to fill in the gap between the various kinds of models that we can make and our data if we overcome the primitivism of most present techniques of data collection, measurement, and, in particular, design, and build up a collection of empirical findings about system processes within organizations. Once we have a body of propositions about organizations as social systems and the functions of role expectations, visibility, communication, styles of leadership, and peer group norms, and approximate quantitative values for such variables, we can begin to fit them into models that can actually predict something. Good models require good empirical research.

One of the more successful simulation models was developed by William McPhee at the Bureau of Applied Social Research. This model generated voting behavior on the basis of social group membership, peer group influence, and the issues raised by the campaign.[15] It was used in the analysis of the 1960 primaries. This model was based upon three earlier studies of elections, in 1940, 1948, and 1950, all of which used the panel method of repeated interviews and obtained data not only on isolated individuals but on their friends, family, and fellow workers. All the studies were thus able to describe the social processes of contact, the arousal of interest, influence, and decision-making that occur within a community during a campaign. This empirical base of three studies over ten years, each study building its methods and hypotheses on the ones before, enabled McPhee to set up a

**14.** Peter Blau, *et al.,* "The Structure of Small Bureaucracies," *American Sociological Review,* XXXI. (1966), 179-191.
**15.** W. N. McPhee, "Note on a Campaign Simulator," in *Formal Theories of Mass Behavior,"* ed. William McPhee (New York: The Free Press, 1963), pp. 169-183.

workable model. This same method should be applied to organizational behavior.

Qualitative studies have played and will continue to play a crucial role in suggesting concepts and relationships; a good quantitative study cannot be done without careful exploratory research that presents some ideas about how things work in the system under study. Quantitative studies then provide empirical generalizations that can go into "propositional inventories." Axiomatic theory and model building organize propositions and generate ideas of system processes and these, in turn, direct further systematic empirical research. This is the ideal of science. Given simulation models and mathematical models that integrate a set of propostions, we can generate new propositions for empirical research that we might never have thought of as long as we were restricted to lists of two-variable propositions.

Since there are many people here today from large organizations, I would particularly like to urge the necessity of cooperation between university research institutes and business and governmental organizations in providing access to organizational settings for research. It is apparently easier to get a scientist to the moon than to get a social scientist into a big city school system these days. Columbia researchers have better luck getting to the bottom of the Mariana trench than studying the operation of a network news department. It took the crisis of a presidential assassination to get access to two of the three major networks. It is not difficult to raise the money necessary for such studies as I have suggested, yet these studies will be possible only if a relationship of continuing cooperation with large organizations can be established.

## ALVIN F. ZANDER

*Professor of Psychology and Director, Research Center for Group Dynamics, University of Michigan.* Professor Zander has been a member of the University of Michigan faculty since 1948. He has served as a program director in the Research Center for Group Dynamics (1948-1959) and has been its director since 1959. Prior to this he was a postdoctoral fellow at the University of Iowa (1942-1943); assistant to the research director, Boy Scouts of America (1943-1944); clinical psychologist in the U. S. Public Health Service and Navy (1944-1946); and assistant professor of psychology at Springfield College (1946-1947). He was a Fulbright Scholar in Oslo, Norway, in 1958-1959.

36

# THE DESIRE FOR GROUP ACHIEVEMENT

We are an achieving society. We seek a sense of accomplishment. We set goals for ourselves, work toward these goals and often ask ourselves, "What have I accomplished?" A good deal of what we value—and a good deal of the strain—comes about because we are strivers.

In an organization, we work for the achievement of our group. Do we feel the same sense of accomplishment when the group reaches a goal as when we personally reach one? Do we have a sense of failure for our groups? The answer to both questions is almost certainly yes. But we know distressingly little about how organizations set their goals; particularly, we know very little about how the desire to achieve and the value of success affect the way organizations go about setting their goals.

Some organizations are required to set goals—the United Fund, for instance—and many units in a large organization are required to establish quotas having to do with scrap loss, profit, the use of manpower, and the like. The members of the organization, moreover, desire to know what their goals are, and if they don't know, they invent them. For example, if we asked someone what his job was, he could easily tell us. He would say that in part he worked to fulfill the expectations of his colleagues, but he would also say that his job served a particular function within the group. He would assert that his work advanced some larger purpose. In a recent study of a chemical firm, we asked the workers what dissatisfied them most about their jobs. The most frequent answer was that they were not certain that their jobs contributed toward the organization's goals.

It is known that people become more involved if they have a say in determining their goals. Various group-decision experiments demonstrate that people more often follow through on a decision reached by the group. The writings of people like Likert,[1] McGregor,[2] and Marrow[3] emphasize the importance, as they see it, of giving employees a chance to participate in setting the goals for their groups. Progressive education has come to the world of business.

We note in many writings that subgroups within a larger organization typically select goals that are unique to them and that may be more or less relevant to the larger goals of the organization. Stanley Seashore, in a study of the standards of a number of small groups within a firm, observed that the more the members of a subgroup liked their managers, the more likely it was that the subgroup's particular goals were in accord with the larger goals of the organization.[4]

Subgroups often set their own goals at a level different from and more attainable than those of the larger society because they cannot achieve what that society requires of them. This is a current explanation of why boys form gangs and create unique values quite different from those in our society.

The most important criterion for group goal-setting is created when a group engages in the same task a number of times and has some evidence after each trial about how well the group has performed. This evidence arouses an expectation of what the group will be able to do the next time, and this expectation becomes goal-like in the sense that members evaluate the group's subsequent performances in relation to it.

In thinking about the motives of members, we need to separate four interrelated ideas:

First, there are the individual goals that people bring into an organization, the personal demands they place upon themselves as a result of their training, professional associations, or whatever.

Second, there are kinds of goals that a member would prefer his group to have. One man's preference may be quite different from another's.

**1.** R. Likert, *New Patterns of Management* (New York: McGraw-Hill, 1959).
**2.** D. McGregor, *The Human Side of Enterprise* (New York: McGraw-Hill, 1959).
**3.** A. Marrow, *Making Management Human* (New York: McGraw-Hill, 1957).
**4.** S. Seashore, *Group Cohesiveness in the Industrial Work Group* (Ann Arbor, Michigan: Institute for Social Research, 1954).

Third, there is the goal for the set, the group goal. This is what a collection of people, after exchanging views, has chosen as an appropriate goal for the unit.

Fourth, there is the group's goal for the member. This is the goal that the group, once it has decided upon a particular level of aspiration, requires of a given member.

These separate ideas are in a circular, causal sequence, and if we change any one of them, we are likely to create consequences for the others. The two that I am most interested in here are the members' goal for the group and the group's goal; and primarily, but not exclusively, I will be concerned with the type of goal that the members have a say in establishing.

From research on the selection of group goals, we have formulated ten generalizations, which fall into three categories: the effects of goals on group behavior; factors influencing goal selection; and performance and evaluation.[5]

## GOALS AND GROUP BEHAVIOR

**1. A group goal generates particular behavior among members.** This is a full grasp of the obvious. But it is important to recognize that a group without a goal behaves quite differently from one that has a goal.

In training activities, we sometimes place a set of strangers around a table, give them no purpose, and ask them to decide what they wish to do. Grown-up men in such a situation become remarkably inept. They giggle, they apologize for every suggestion they make, they listen to one another half-heartedly and they have difficulty in deciding anything. Yet, when we give the same set of people a definite assignment, they soon decide what each must do in order to work effectively toward that goal. They have entirely different personalities in the two settings.

Rewards also affect group behavior. Assume that we offer a single reward to one group for doing well as a group, that we tell another group each member will be rewarded if he does well, and that to a third we say nothing about rewards at all. In the group with a single reward for the unit, members recognize their interdependent relationship and trust each other. They are more receptive to each other's ideas and are better able to influence one another, according to findings of a study made twenty years ago by Morton Deutsch.[6] A more recent study by Edwin Thomas led to the additional finding that members develop stronger feelings of responsibilitiy for the group's fate in a common-reward situation.[7] They know who is expecting what of them, and thus they perform better. They perform so well, in fact, that they become tense in their efforts to reach their goal because they come close to their ceiling of ability. What's more, they like one another more as a result of having a group goal.

**2. Clearly defined goals generate more effective effort than unclear goals.** I illustrate this for students by dividing them up into small groups and giving each group a very difficult and complicated topic to discuss. Usually it is a very abstract issue, feeds back on itself, and sounds like something teachers talk about at a convention. The students' discussion of this topic is marked by interruption, wandering,

**5.** A. Zander, "Group Aspirations," in *Group Dynamics, Research and Theory,* ed. D. Cartwright and A. Zander (New York: Harper & Row, 1968).
**6.** M. Deutsch, "The Effects of Cooperation and Competition upon Group Process." *Human Relations,* II (1949), 129-152, 199-231.
**7.** E. J. Thomas, "Effects of Facilitative Role Interdependence on Group Functioning." *Human Relations,* X (1957), 347-366.

and a great deal of confusion. After they have stumbled over the complex subject for a little while, I give them a very simple topic, like listing the names of all of the organizations in the campus community. They go to work on the simple topic at once. The amount of effective effort increases because they understand what they are trying to do.

A couple of researchers were able, in a small group setting, to give separate groups either a very clear task or an unclear task. In observing how the groups behaved in these two contrasting situations, they noted that the people were a good deal more interested in the task when they knew what they were doing. They had a greater feeling of belonging to the group, they got along better, and they were more willing to accept one another's influence.

Goals vary in their scope. Some goals are so broad and so vaguely defined that it is difficult to specify the best way to work toward them. March and Simon have called these goals "nonoperational."[8] The other day I was reading a study of the goal structure of the present Mexican government. The goals specified were to attain political stability, increase economic growth, improve the public welfare, and Mexicanize the society. These are fine goals, but how should the government go about them, and how will it know when it has attained them?

Every large organization has nonoperational goals, more commonly called "purposes." Seashore, in studying organizations that have a number of objectives, noted that these organizations could describe as many as six to eight separate "important" goals.[9] Seashore thinks these goals should be given degrees of priority, and that the highest priority should be given to those that the majority agrees come closer to the organization's broader purposes.

A few years ago we confirmed the value of working toward a "purpose" through more immediate "goals" when we studied a set of aircraft crews who were being trained in escape and survival. For the final examination, each man was provided with a blanket and compass, and the crews were left in the Sierra Nevadas. The crews were told they had four days to reach a certain geographical point. Before the trek began, we had the members fill out questionnaires. From these data we learned how important each man thought this trek was to his whole career, and we found that the higher the group rated this activity, the better the group performed. In other words, the group worked better when the members considered the immediate, clearly defined goal to be part of a broader, less specific purpose.

There is also merit, however, in leaving some goals minimally defined. In some situations, it is not worth the difficulty involved to get a precise definition; but more than that, loosely defined goals allow a good deal of creative interpretation, which can change as experience requires.

## INFLUENCES ON GOAL SELECTION
The next four generalizations refer to the external and internal factors influencing members in their selection of goals.

   **1. Members prefer their group to have the goal with the greatest uncertainty of achievement.** As individuals, we prefer to avoid tasks that are too easy because they are no challenge to us and to avoid

**8.** J. March and H. Simon, *Organizations* (New York: Wiley, 1957).
**9.** S. Seashore, "Criteria of Organizational Effectiveness," *Michigan Business Review,* XVII (1965), 26-30.

tasks that are too hard because they are frustrating. We tend to favor goals that we have about a fifty-fifty chance of reaching.

In our society, however, success in a difficult task is valued more than success in an easy task and is rewarded more. We can derive from this that people not only choose goals on the basis of what they think they can accomplish; they also take into consideration how attractive the reward is likely to be. They want to be successful on the most difficult task possible for them.

We can study matters like this in the laboratory by giving groups a series of trials on a collective task, asking after each trial, "What do you think your group will be able to do next time?" Everybody does exactly the same thing at exactly the same moment. There is no leader of the group; the group functions as a unit. By having groups engage in this kind of activity, we can make certain observations.

First, groups change their goals quite readily in this setting. After a success, they tend to raise their goals; after a failure, they tend to lower their goals. This suggests that when they see how well they have done, they think they can probably do at least that well next time. The attractiveness of attempting a higher, more difficult goal becomes evident, too, because successful groups raise their goals more often than failing groups lower theirs. And successful groups raise their goals more than failing groups lower them.

If we tell groups to start at a certain level, very difficult or very easy, they don't move very far from that level. But people who are assigned difficult tasks like their tasks better than people assigned easy tasks, suggesting again that working on a difficult task is more attractive than working on an easy one.

In one experiment, we gave some groups a "progress report" after each trial so they knew how well they were doing. We found that when we gave other groups no evidence about how they were progressing, these groups assumed they were successful and would choose a more difficult level for their next attempt. Their choice of more difficult goals exactly matched those of groups who had succeeded on every trial. No news here is taken to be good news.

Richard Emerson, a sociologist who went along on the Mount Everest climb, got some interesting data to demonstrate that groups desire to keep their anticipation of the outcome uncertain.[10] Emerson carried out his study by making standard comments and recording the responses. If he made an optimistic remark about how things were going, "Look, we are way ahead of schedule," he would get a negative response: "Yes, but we've got a long way to go yet," or "That looks like a storm brewing." In contrast, if he made a negative remark, he would be likely to get an optimistic response, so that his push in one direction was countered by a push in the opposite direction. Many studies have been done in recent years comparing the risk-taking of individuals and groups. Wallach, Kogan, and Bem provided support for a conclusion that is important to management: people arrive at much riskier decisions as a group than as individuals.[11] By a "risky" decision, we mean one more difficult to attain, or one that is more likely to have negative consequences if it fails.

**2. The more members have a desire for group achievement, the more likely the group is to choose goals of intermediate difficulty.** Desire for group achievement is a situational motivation created when a person finds himself a member of a group being asked to

**10.** R. Emerson, "Mount Everest: A Case Study of Communication Feed Back and Sustained Group Goal Striving," *Sociometry*, XXIX (1966), 213-227.
**11.** M. Wallach, et al., "Group Influence on Individual Risk-taking," *Journal of Abnormal and Social Psychology*, LX (1962), 75-86.

Alvin F. Zander

perform against some standard of excellence. What each member has in mind is not so much to attain success, but to attain the consequences of success, the feeling of satisfaction following group achievement.

We can create a desire for group achievement experimentally. When we do this, our general prediction is that groups in which we create a higher desire for achievement will be more likely to choose intermediate goals than other groups. These are the goals with a 50-50 chance of success, the maximally uncertain ones. In one situation, we assigned a task in which the group could achieve nothing unless a central member performed his activity first. The central person, thus, had a greater desire for group achievement. Comparing his goals for the group with those of the more peripheral members, we found that he preferred more intermediate level tasks, while peripheral members preferred tasks away from the intermediate range.

In a subsequent experiment, we created strong groups and weak groups. We created strong groups by having the members choose a name for their group, by emphasizing to them that they *were* a group, and by telling them that we had data about them individually that suggested they would work well together. A weak group was created by having the members sit behind screens so they could not see one another and emphasizing the fact of their separation. We gave their group a number instead of letting them choose a name and told them that our data suggested that they might not work well together.

After these preliminaries, we seated all groups behind screens

46

where they had no opportunity for communication with their co-members. We had them work on a series of tasks, giving them a choice of any level of group difficulty they wished. The strong groups most often chose tasks in the intermediate range, while the weak groups chose either very low or very high goals. The strong groups had a greater desire to achieve success.

**3. The more fearful the group is of failure, the more it will avoid the middle range and select unreasonably high goals.** We can experimentally create a fear of the consequences of failing as we created the earlier desire for group achievement. In one situation, which we call a "reward condition," we tell the members that the more difficult the level they work on, the better the reward for success. We say nothing about what would happen if they failed. To create a "cost condition," in which the group's fear of failure will be heightened, we give them the reward first and tell them that every time they fail, we will take away some of the reward; moreover, the easier the task failed the more reward is to be taken away. Making failure on an easier task more negative than failure on a more difficult task conforms to the usual values in our society.

Our prediction was that the people in the cost setting would prefer very difficult tasks more than the people in the reward setting, and the results of the experiment supported it.

In another instance, we created groups of people who had a high anxiety about taking tests and contrasted them with groups who had little of this fear. We found that groups of people who are fearful of taking tests are more likely to choose very difficult group tasks, whereas those with little anxiety are more likely to choose the intermediate range. Thus, fear of failure generates a selection of unreasonably difficult goals, which generates further failure.

Many of us were taught to "hitch our wagon to a star," but we are more likely to do this if we fear the consequences of failure. If we set ourselves a very high goal and don't attain it, we can say, "Oh, well. Who could?" and our friends can say, "Well, you gave it a good try, though." Failure to reach a more difficult goal is less embarrassing than failure to reach an easier goal.

We have compiled some data on the effects of failure on goal setting in a study of United Fund campaigns in 150 communities over a four-year period. Communities with four failures in a row set their goals for the fourth year far beyond what their past three levels of performance indicated they could possibly attain. In contrast, communities that had three successes in a row, then a failure, set goals for the fourth year only slightly higher than their past level.

**4. External agents influence group members strongly in their choice of goals.** The United Fund, for instance, has a great deal of outside pressure on it: the users of the money want the goals to go up; the givers of the money want the goals to go down.

In the laboratory, we told our experimental groups that we had set up a committee to decide the goal levels for each group. We told some groups that if they performed up to the expectations of the committee, they would be rewarded; we told other groups that if they did not meet the committee's expectations, there would be certain negative consequences. In both instances, the groups paid relatively little attention to their past scores and set their goals to conform to the committee's decision, regardless of how unreasonable those goals might have been.

Furthermore, if we tell one group while they are working on a task what other groups are doing, the group uses this information, not their past performance levels, to determine its future goals.

In another study of this kind we created a "policy committee." This three-man team sat in the experiment room, watching the groups work. The "committee" knew the tasks of the workers and how well they were doing trial by trial. Between trials, we asked the committee how well it thought each group would do on the next trial. This estimate was then to be delivered to the workers, as evidence of what other people thought they could do.

However, the actual estimates made by the observers were not in fact delivered. Since we wanted each group to get exactly the same message, we substituted our own messages. Some groups' potentials were evaluated too high and some too low, but everyone paid more attention to the outside opinion than to his own judgment or the group's past performance levels.

Interestingly enough, the "policy committee" selected almost exactly the same goals for the groups—before our sleight-of-hand—that the groups selected for themselves. When we tried to influence the policy makers' judgment by telling them what similar committees did, it did not have any effect; neither did telling them that they would benefit if the observed group did well. Perhaps policymakers are able to operate rationally, and set goals more rationally, than the people who are working for the goal.

These data imply that groups, perhaps more than individuals, do not exist for themselves alone. They come into existence largely because they are of some service to the environment, to the larger organization, or to needs of the individual members that can be better met by united actions. Thus, groups often have to give up autonomy and accept pressure from the environment to perform in a particular fashion.

## PERFORMANCE AND EVALUATION

The four remaining generalizations have to do with group performance, how it is evaluated, and how performance affects members' desire to continue as a group.

**1. Goal level determines the level of the group's performance.** We might assume this as a matter of fact, but it isn't always so. Research on group performance is quite a mixture of findings, and surprisingly the relation of performance to goal has rarely been studied.

One study relevant to this question was done in the General Electric Company, where foremen were given various levels of performance for their subgroups to achieve.[12] Some foremen were given impossible levels; some were given "challenging levels," that is, a little bit higher than they had reached in the past; and some were given very easy tasks. The test period covered six months, and the testers found that the subgroups with the "challenging" (middle level) tasks performed much better than those who had either the easy or the impossible tasks.

**2. Groups judge their performance by the goals they have set.** After each experiment, we asked each member to evaluate his group's performance. It is no surprise to discover that if the group managed to accomplish its objective, the member tended to rate the group very high. This was a consistent practice, whether the goals were imposed on the group, the goal was ridiculously low, or the members were influenced by any of the factors mentioned earlier. This same criterion applied to failing groups. It didn't matter that the goal might have been unreasonably high; members decided their adequacy and their group esteem on the basis of whether or not they achieved the goal.

**3. A member rates himself by his group's score, if he is important within the group.** The civil rights movement has asserted that being a member of a minority group has unfortunate consequences for an individual. We know, however, that this isn't always true, because some members of minority groups have very good self-esteem. The question is, under what conditions do members of a group allow the group's reputation to rub off on them as individuals?

In the experiment described earlier, where we had a central figure carrying the peripheral members, the central man was much more likely to rate himself as a success if his group succeeded and as a failure if the group failed. The peripheral people, on the other hand, rated themselves favorably regardless of what the group did. They were on the border of the group; the group's behavior was something that somebody else was responsible for.

**12.** A. C. Stedry and M. Kay, *The Effects of Goal Difficulty on Performance* (Crotonville, New York: Management Development and Employee Relations Services, General Electric Company, 1964).

Alvin F. Zander

Members with higher test anxiety were much less aware of what the group was doing than those with little test anxiety. It was as though they didn't know what was going on because they were so concerned with themselves. People like this are also much more likely to rate themselves by what they do individually than by the group's score.

A group is a handy thing to have around: if the group fails, you can ignore it; if it succeeds, you can take credit for it when you are a peripheral member.

**4. If a group succeeds and achieves favorable consequences, members react favorably to the experience.** After these experiments we asked participants what they thought of the test, using such questions as: Was it a valid test? Would you like to take it again? How important was it? How hard did you try? Those who attained their level of aspiration usually gave approving answers on these matters; those who performed poorly usually gave negative answers. Groups that do not perform well and then get another task to carry out have ways of avoiding the negative consequences of failure, the easiest being to resist trying the task again.

**CONCLUSION**
We have tried to apply our understanding of individual motivation to group settings and come up with an understanding of group motivation. There are still many questions we need to answer. We need to know more about dealing with goal conflicts: What do groups do when striving for one goal makes it difficult to accomplish another?

*Alvin F. Zander*

We should know about conditions under which goals facilitate or are detrimental to performance. We need to understand more about the desire for group achievement; we are currently developing a test to detect this characteristic in people. It would be helpful if we understood more about the relative weight of personal goals and group goals in determining the individual's behavior as a group member.

These questions, then, are still open, and point the direction for future research in group motivational processes.

**ABRAHAM ZALEZNIK**

*Professor of Organizational Behavior, Graduate School of Business Administration, Harvard University.* Professor Zaleznik has served as a faculty member of the Atlantic Summer School of Advanced Business Administration, Halifax, Nova Scotia (1953, 1954, and 1955); the Advanced Management Program of the Far East, Baguio, Philippines (1958 and 1959); and the Advanced Management Seminar of Keio University, Japan (1958, 1964, and 1965). He is also a consultant to various companies and government agencies.

54

# EXTERNAL AND INTERNAL ROLE CONFLICT

An understanding of executive role conflict and how it affects actions of the executive, both within and without the organizational structure, is crucial in applying behavioral science to industry. The executive is expected to play many roles, to wear many hats; barriers to action or conflicting role requirements often create serious external —real—and internal—neurotic—conflicts for the executive. It is my intention to present brief explanations of these two forms of conflict, giving greater emphasis to internal conflicts because I believe that most conflicts originate as problems attached to inner motives and defenses. Finally, I shall pose several questions for the consideration of those who are studying executive behavior.

55

*Abraham Zaleznik*

## External Conflict

External conflict can be defined as opposition between the person and his environment, or some aspect of his environment which is a barrier or restriction to action. For example, two vice presidents of an organization aspire to become president, but since there can be only one president, there is an external conflict for each. Conflicts also occur when a person wants something which can be achieved only by losing something else. Retirement means the breaking of bonds between the executive and certain gratifying activities, and this sense of loss or deprivation produces conflict. Furthermore, if an executive wants something but does not know how to achieve it, this may cause considerable distress and frustration. Limited financial resources, for example, hinder new organizational programs, thus causing external conflicts.

These examples of conflict involve an actual barrier or separation which the executive must overcome to achieve his goal. However, there is another form of external conflict which is related to the concept of role. An executive occupies a position in the organization, and other people, other position holders in this structure, have prior expectations as to how this person should act. His boss, for example, expects him to get out production and to meet objectives. His actions are measured, therefore, against a criterion of performance. Subordinates, on the other hand, expect him to show consideration and treat them as human beings. These two conflicting demands, to be concerned with performance and to show consideration, are called *initiating structure versus consideration.*[1] The occupant of a position must perform certain kinds of work, but pressures from other position holders may affect the way in which it is done.

Richard Neustadt, in *Presidential Power*,[2] makes the point that the essence of the U.S. presidency is that other people want to get things done through the Number One Man. In other words, they want things from him. The story goes that Franklin Roosevelt handled this problem in a simple way. If he thought that someone was coming to ask him for something which he did not want to give or could not respond to, he would talk for the course of the entire interview. At the end of it, he would shake the man's hand and say, "It was so good of you to come to see me, please drop in again when you are in town." The visitor would leave, thinking that he had had a nice talk, and only later would it occur to him that he had come to ask for something but never quite got around to doing this. Roosevelt had manipulated the situation in order to avoid saying "no"; his friendly manner obscured these tactics.

External conflicts of many types face the executive in his day-to-day work or long-range planning and make demands on the ego to perform work. Often, such conflicts may produce frustration, anxiety, or tension. However, this kind of distress is a very normal and usual accompaniment of work. By no means would we assume that this type of crisis is connected to any conflicts that he has experienced earlier in life. Nor would we say that these conflicts are pathological or that the person who encounters them is deviant. Instead, we would say that this is the nature of life, and everyone has to deal with such situations.

**1.** The early Michigan studies dealt with the problem from the standpoint of the production-centered executive versus the person-centered executive and tried to show the relationship between them. See: E. A. Fleishman, *et al.*, *Leadership and Supervision in Industry* (Columbus: Bureau of Educational Research, Ohio State University, 1955) See also: Talcott Parsons and R. F. Bales, *Family, Socialization and Interaction Process* (Glencoe, Illinois: Free Press, 1955).
**2.** Richard E. Neustadt, *Presidential Power* (New York: New American Library, 1964).

*Abraham Zaleznik*

## Internal Conflict

The most distressful conflicts, however, are those in which a person faced with a problem places it in the context of the whole range of life issues with which he has been dealing. This brings me, then, to the major area I wish to discuss — the nature of neurotic inner conflict, what we understand about it now, and how it relates to major issues in the life of the executive.

Man continually lives within the matrix of conflicting energy processes which may or may not bear any objective relationship to events in his environment. The opposition of these forces creates inner, or neurotic, conflict, and this in turn makes a demand on the ego to perform work. The way in which the ego experiences this may take a very virulent form, such as anxiety or some disturbance in function — insomnia, the impulse to act, the strong pressure to do something which may not be relevant to the problem. Even more significant, the demand that work be performed may lead the person to seek intervention from outside in order to solve the problem.

The basic model of opposing forces within the personality is that of a wish versus a restriction. There is something I want, some gratification which I desire, but the restriction of conscience, most likely, says this gratification is not permitted. This tends to create an impasse and causes the ego either to transform the wish into a form which is acceptable to the conscience, to bury the wish to prevent the energy from being discharged in action, or to cope with it in some other way.

This perspective on inner conflict comes mainly from the psycho-analytic study of personality developed by Sigmund Freud. Originally a method for treating ill people, it has become an instrument for research and study of the human personality in order to help explain how individuals develop and why they act the way they do. In doing this, psychoanalysis considers both biological processes and the changing role and relationship of objects in the environment to the person. Moreover, psychoanalytic psychology stresses the idea of the prototypical crisis, or life issue, which is essential to the individual's development at a given time and which reappears in his life context again and again.

An example of a prototypical issue is the famous Oedipus complex. The metaphorical reference to the tragedy of Oedipus refers to the notion that between the ages of three and five the male child experiences a strong antipathy toward his father in addition to a strong and neurotic attachment to his mother. The evidence suggests that one way this problem is solved is by learning to delay or to put aside these aggressions and fantasies in the interests of reality and to identify with the male model. However, a prototypical issue is never totally resolved and may recur during successive stages of development.

Returning to the example of two executives who aspire to become president of a company, this opposition may be treated as an external conflict. However, suppose that for one vice president the rivalry over who is going to be number one becomes entangled with the subconscious Oedipus complex, and he begins to say to himself, "Do I want it because I want to knock him off? If I get it, is something going to happen to him?" This inner conflict causes anxiety and tension and may even lead to action, as for example in an altruistic mood he were to say, "I don't really want to be president; I'll let him have it, and I will support him." What was originally an external conflict has become attached to a prototypical crisis and is now an internal conflict.

The theme of Shakespeare's *Macbeth* illustrates a second prototypical situation. An ambitious nobleman, Macbeth, murdered the King of Scotland, Duncan. However, as Duncan's successor, Macbeth trusted no one, fearing that he also would be murdered. He became a lonely, embittered man, and this ultimately led to his destruction. It can be said that his past actions and present situation suddenly fused and became one. The objects in the present were no longer independent in their own right, but representatives of the past, therefore causing intense anxiety and tension.

Technically speaking, an inner conflict of this nature is referred to as a *repetition compulsion.* The individual is forced to repeat old conflicts from the past in the present. Compelled by problems experienced in the past which have not been solved adequately, he is unable to gratify wishes or to placate a bad conscience.

A good example of this in the field of executive leadership is the case of Woodrow Wilson. There is a very interesting book by Alexander and Juliette George on Wilson's career as an executive.[3] Basically the authors demonstrate that in his various executive positions, as president of Princeton University, Governor of the State of New Jersey, and President of the United States, Wilson experienced conflicts which seemed to be external. For example, he wanted to establish a certain graduate school at Princeton, but Dean West opposed it; when President, his plan for the League of Nations was opposed by Henry Cabot Lodge. The uncanny similarities among these conflicts suggest that he was trying to relive and solve the same problem. The Georges suggest that this was an internal conflict, a repetition compulsion.

Fusion of the past and present can also involve a *transference of emotions* from people in the past, usually parents, to those in the present. Persons in present life situations stand as symbols or representatives of figures from the past who have meant a great deal to the individual. For example, in the case study of Wilson, the hypothesis the authors propose is that Wilson's transference conflicts concerned the nature of his relation to his father. Wilson consciously adored his father, a stern and exacting personality; the Georges assert, however, that there were underlying negative feelings toward the father which were transferred unconsciously to West and then Lodge, thus contributing to the conflict with these two men.

In the world of the executive, the boss tends to become the father symbol, and subordinates seek approval or justification of themselves as human beings by this important figure. In addition, a man's wife may not be entirely a person in her own right, but may actually stand as a symbol for a mother or sister. The present figure is then asked to perform as the one who will justify, who will make right that which

3. Alexander L. George and Juliette L. George, *Woodrow Wilson and Colonel House: A Personality Study* (New York: Dover Publications, 1956).

one feels had been wrong, and who will act out a meaningful conflict from the past.

Furthermore, it is important to recognize that without a good, quantitatively significant dose of self-confidence the executive will be torn by others' demands which are in opposition to his own desires, and thus be rendered unable to make decisions. At one time, anyone having a high regard for himself was considered to be a self-centered and bad person. The myth of Narcissus—who went to a pool, looked in, and seeing his image, fell in love with it—was used to illustrate this idea. I am suggesting now that we review and rethink the role of egoism.

On the one hand, it is clear that the executive does need a good, healthy amount of self-confidence. But on the other hand, if he were to say, "I need no one, because I love only myself," he might be involved in self-deprivation or withdrawal which would markedly impair his ability to solve problems. There are four areas of conflict in the executive's life in which egoism, or the lack of it, can be crucial. They could be labeled *getting and giving, controlling and being controlled, competing and cooperating,* and *producing and facilitating.* Let us look briefly at each.

**Getting and giving.** The person who occupies a position of responsibility often feels that all he does in life is to provide for others, but that no one, in turn, does this for him. He begins to experience a sense of yearning or melancholy, or even to think that he is being cheated. He might have had the illusion that if one occupies a responsible position many interesting pleasures and privileges go along with it. Instead, he learns that other people make demands on him, they want things; the executive may say to himself, "Is this what I fought for?"

On the other hand, he may experience this conflict as an intense feeling that he is getting too much, that his position is something he really does not deserve. Consequently, he may enter into a state of self-denial, allowing himself no pleasures. Such a person will not even take a vacation because of the compulsion to continue working. Others may reward him for this self-denial, seeing him as a responsible, altruistic person; they do not realize that an intense inner conflict actually motivates his hard work.

The conflict between getting and giving for the executive may also appear in his family life. At work he is active, aggressive, and responsible, but when he comes home he may become passive, compliant, and relatively uncommunicative. What he is trying to do is to fall into a pattern of dependency, with the net result that his actions do not provide satisfactory relationships with his wife or children. Tensions in the life of the family may stem from his yearning for a passive role.

There is some evidence to suggest that crises over getting and giving occur mostly in the mid-career years. I am sure you are familiar with the story of the executive who has lived the exemplary life, has done everything that is expected of him and more; yet, when he reaches the mid-forties, he suddenly knocks it all over. He goes to a tropical island paradise and becomes a beachcomber, or he may even embezzle money in an outbreak of unexpected, rash behavior. In other cases, this conflict takes the form of a severe depression.

From these examples it is evident that the executive must work out a satisfactory balance between getting and giving. It is just as false for him to provide completely for others as it is for him to be a leaner and have other people provide for him.

**Controlling and being controlled.** There is evidence to suggest that all of us in the early years, and then later in life, go through a period in which we believe in magical control. The youngster who turns himself around, gets dizzy, stops, points his finger out, and says, "Stop, world." He waits a minute, and the world stops. He feels as if he were invested with great powers because he made the world turn, and he made it stop.

In the course of the life of the executive, he may act out the fantasy that he causes the world to turn and that he also causes it to stop. Once he begins to think that this is the way life is, he plays a most dangerous game. If you want to know the nature of the dangers, I would suggest you read the biography of James Forrestal, who lost perspective on what he was doing and came to a very tragic end.[4]

However, the executive who sees only the complexities may endure them out of a sense of helplessness. To feel that he can cause nothing to happen and can stop nothing is equally false. Helplessness is a pathological reaction to the realization that one cannot control or have everything.

In its earliest form, the problem of control is related to the problem of loss and restitution. That is, when the individual psychologically experiences certain losses, in his efforts at restitution he may engage in this duel between omnipotence and helplessness, thus not working out a satisfactory in-between or integrated solution. In other words, there should be a reasonable attitude toward control. There are certain things the executive can handle, and there are other things he cannot.

**Competing and cooperating.** This third area involves a conflict between egoism and responding to the needs of the organization and of others. The basic issue is one of self-confidence. The person must learn to feel like an executive, to "feel secure" in the judgments which he makes. The tendency to stress cooperation, doing what is good for others, as I have indicated in terms of achieving a higher purpose, does not take adequate account of the importance of individual goals. The executive must be aware of personal goals which are separate from goals of the organization and of other persons and use these goals for his own achievement and gratification.

However, if a person stresses his own goals and inclinations too strongly, he will run into opposition from others who think differently and desire other things. The executive must have a sufficient quantity of aggression to support what he feels is personally right. Here, the issue of power is relevant to understanding the nature of competition and cooperation, since to "compete" means essentially to mobilize authority into power and to actively persuade people that one is right.

Many organizational studies emphasize the need for cooperation.

**4.** A. A. Rogow, *James Forrestal* (New York: Macmillan, 1963).

That is, if you occupy a position in the structure which gives you power and potential to influence other people, the thing for you to do is to give it away in the form of certain rituals or practices, like delegations or committees. I think we need to turn our attention to what makes for competition. How does it work; when is it successful; how does the individual assert himself to say, "This is what I think should be done"? How does he convince other people, either individually or in groups?

**Producing and facilitating.** Essentially, this relates to the problem of the active versus the passive method of experiencing oneself at work. The evidence is quite strong that many persons are inhibited at work. Inhibitions occur when the person becomes overly concerned with self-justification in the form of the question: "Am I adequate as a man?" This preoccupation with adequacy can take the active form of compulsive work in an effort to use productivity as a means of self-justification. The opposite of this active form is seen in the passive form of acting as a "talent scout" or catalyst who facilitates the productive work of others while remaining anonymously in the background. The former runs the danger of becoming a ritual which prevents self-development and avoids new experiences and challenges. The passive form leads to disappointment and anxiety about lost goals and aspirations. I think we must understand how this relates to the life of the executive. Once again we need an appropriate balance between activity and passivity which relates more deeply to the problems and the concerns of the individual executive.

## Questions for Consideration

In light of the ideas which I have just presented, the following questions indicate additional areas which need consideration. First, if you take the distinction between external and internal conflict, and if you are willing to go along with the notion that the whole area of inner conflict has to be studied more carefully, would it be fair for me to conclude that in the study of executive behavior today, excessive emphasis has been placed on structural solutions? By structural solutions I am referring to common solutions such as changing the organizational chart; it actually may be more important to see the significance of inner conflict in relation to causative factors in organizational problems.

Second, has emphasis been placed on ideological solutions which seek to attach people to certain values—cooperation, democracy, permissiveness—which really are not solutions at all?

Third, has emphasis been placed on asking people to adopt a leadership style or pattern which is based on an external model and not on their own inner strength? Are we doing a disservice to the cause of executive development by telling people to be like Model A, Model B, or Model C when the real essence of executive development is for the individual to learn to take account of himself, to lead from strength and build out from what he can do, and to have a job which is unique to himself?

Fourth, is there an inadequate treatment in research of executive behavior within a time perspective? That is, we tend to look at the executive in the here and now, cross-sectionally, and in terms of his relationship with others. We pay inadequate attention to the issue of individual development, and therefore, to how a man deals with the inner and outer problems which he faces. I suggest that in the absence of an historical perspective, we have a two-dimensional picture.

Fifth, is too little attention given to the deeper issues suggested in the polarities I have talked about or to the way the individual shifts and alters his position in response to biological as well as social and individual changes?

**ROBERT L. KAHN**

*Program Director, Survey Research Center, University of Michigan.* Before joining the faculty of the University of Michigan, Professor Kahn served with the U. S. Bureau of Census, where he was acting chief of the field division.

70

# THE OPEN SYSTEM AND ROLE CONFLICT

The open system approach to organization is a very broad subject, and I will try to describe it only briefly, by way of background. Then I will discuss role conflict, in a way that illustrates the open system approach to one limited aspect of organizational life. Lastly, I want to suggest some approaches to the management of conflict in organization, since I concur with Professor Zaleznik's view that the elimination of conflict is not a realistic—or even desirable—goal.

With that three-point agenda in mind, let us consider, first, what we mean by an "open system."

71

*Robert L. Kahn*

## THE OPEN SYSTEM

Any organization involves certain recurring processes, and these processes involve certain inputs—for example, raw materials and sources of power in such forms as steam or electricity, and people. Furthermore, the term system implies by definition that some work is being done, something is being transformed. Raw inputs are combined or separated, rearranged or altered, or changed into a form and moved to a place that makes them more useful. The fact that they are useful —that is, to be used—reminds us that the organization is always engaged in a process of output or export. Whatever is transformed within the organization has to be absorbed, accepted, by some outside agency.

It is this cycle of input, transformation, and output that I have in mind when I talk about an open system. The organization is dependent on the environment to absorb its outputs and to indicate that they are acceptable by giving the organization what it needs to survive and continue with the process. This is obvious in the case of business, where the customer gives money for the organization's product and that money is used by the organization to renew its supplies and facilities.

It is less obvious, perhaps, in the case of the university; but at the season of the year when state legislatures are deciding on university budgets, some of us, at least, are aware of the fact that the same process goes on for nonprofit organizations, and that it has the same kind of organizational implications for growth and survival.

Still another deduction we can make is that any organization exists

72

only so long as its input is greater than its output. If the organization cannot import energy enough both to turn out its product and keep itself in repair, it runs down—which brings me to the further point of what we mean by an organization's running down.

What we mean has to do with the notion of entropy, which we have borrowed (I hope without doing it too much violence) from physical science. Entropy means simply that the most probable state of matter is random nonarrangement—disorder. When we talk about something running down, we mean that it literally is not organized. (To say that something is organized means that patterns have been created or imposed; order has been created out of randomness.)

Typically, businesses are organized well enough so that we don't relate the notion of entropy to the notion of organization; but for various reasons, voluntary groups more often verge on nonorganization. Meetings may be sparsely attended; objectives often may be unattained; leadership positions may be hard to fill or even go unfilled. Your own experience with the Boy Scouts, the Red Cross, or civic bodies of various kinds may substantiate this description.

What I am suggesting is that entropy is a general tendency in human affairs. It is not likely that an organization will spring into life and be sustained by accident. It takes effort for the organization to overcome the tendency toward entropy and keep itself organized, which is why it has to take in more than it can produce.

This limitation on the ratio of input to output is not unique to large-scale human organizations. It is the kind of thing engineers and physicists think about with respect to any machine. They know that some of the machine's input must be consumed as friction, in order to keep the machine itself in motion. In other words, there is no such thing as complete efficiency in practice.

What I have said up to this point in characterizing an organization as an open system can be said of still larger aggregations, like societies, or smaller ones, like individual biological systems. However, I cannot agree with the general theorists that one theoretical framework can handle all systems "from cell to society." I think that human organizations, although they can be considered open systems, have some unique characteristics; the most important of them, to me, is that the large scale organization, as we encounter it in business or in the academic world, differs from other systems in the nature of its components.

In a machine, we know what the parts are, and even when the machine is stopped or broken, the parts and their connections are still visible. In a biological system, animal or human being, it is again obvious what the parts are, and the parts are visible in death as in life.

When an organization is not in motion, however, somehow the parts are not there. What happens to the organization when people go home at night? Or what happens during a period of strike or change-over? In one sense it exists, but it is no longer visible or tangible. There is a visible shell of buildings and machines, but these are not the organization.

To say that the parts of an organization are people is not satisfying, nor am I willing to agree to it, because people, as Dr. Zaleznik reminded us, are more than parts of organization. I am led to conclude that we organize not people but human acts, patterns of behavior. This means that an organization is unique in that it has a physiology without having an anatomy. It exists only so long as it is in motion, only so long as the expectations of people about how others ought to behave, and the behavior of others in response to the expectations, actually continue.

## ROLE CONFLICT

A role in an organization is a bundle of behaviors that are expected of a person in a particular position, and those behaviors are expected, to a large extent, regardless of who happens to occupy the position.

We can think of an organization as a vast net in which every knot represents an individual office or job, and the strands that connect one knot with another represent bonds of expectation. This means that we get the structure not from the organization chart, as such, nor from piecing together something called formal organization and something called informal organization (which would be everything we couldn't pack into the formal category). Rather, we would pick up this network one knot at a time and ask about each knot, "What are all the other knots to which it is connected, and what is the nature of the connection?" That is, what behavior is expected of the person in this position by people in what other positions?

These groups of interrelated roles are called *role sets; role conflict* means simply the amount of disagreement within a set of people about what the man in the middle should be doing. There would be a role set for every position in the organization, and the job that we were focusing on at any particular moment would be the *focal role*. This doesn't mean that it's important in any particular sense, since each position will be focal when we look at the organization from its point of view.

Taking this view of organization, we can conclude that the usual organization chart is just that special case in which the president's role is the focal one; so, if we want to know how the organization looks from the point of view of everyone in it, we will have to give each person, in turn, the "presidential treatment." This is what we have done in recent studies at the Institute for Social Research.

In a number of companies, we interviewed people in positions from corporate officer to foreman, asking each man to describe the activities he thinks are required in his position and to list the people to whom he is directly related, that is, those doing the requiring. We then interviewed each of these related people and asked them what they think the focal person is doing and what they would like him to do, especially in relation to what he is now doing. Then we went back to the focal person and said, "What messages have you been receiving lately from these various people? What means do they use to communicate with you and to attempt to influence your behavior? What do you think they want you to do?"

This view of organization contrasts with the chain of command shown in the usual organization chart, in that the set of people typically mentioned by a given person includes not only his immediate superior but also his superior once removed, who seems to be in direct touch, despite the chartist convention of showing each echelon linked only to that immediately above it. The organization set of a focal person also includes his immediate subordinates, which is not surprising, as well as people who are adjacent to him in the work flow; and it usually includes one or two or several people whom the chart does not show as having any contact with him at all. These are people for whom the focal person has great respect, or to whom he turns for advice, or whose behavior he uses as a model.

One of the obvious conclusions we reach from looking at organization in this way is that there is no such thing as a job description—that is, one that everybody is necessarily agreed on. Everyone in a role set describes the job of the focal person in relation to his own needs, individual and organizational, and this does not necessarily agree with the job description filed in the personnel department. It might, but the purpose of our research was to see to what extent it did or did not agree, and what the consequences of agreement or disagreement would be. In describing some of the findings of that research, I will be particularly concerned with those cases where the focal person had difficulty reconciling the demands of one member of the role set to those of another. The most familiar example is the case of the foreman whose subordinates say, "Ease off," while his superior says, "Speed up," but this turns out to be only one aspect of a much more complicated picture. In a national survey of some 1,500 people, randomly chosen on a household basis, about half the people interviewed said that they were caught between two or more people or factions. Nine out of ten times, one of the people involved was the boss, but the other factor was much more variable.[1]

---

**1.** For a more complete description, see R. L. Kahn, *et al., Organizational Stress* (New York: Wiley, 1964).

*Robert L. Kahn*

## Coping with Overload

One of the most frequent forms of conflict, and one that we had not expected, turned out to be overload. The person in the middle was in a conflict situation, not because the demands made on him by different people were morally or logically incompatible, but because they could not be done in combination within the constraints of available time. This is an interesting problem, and one that is not typically communicated by the person in the middle to the people who are creating the overload.

Why not? It may be that we think the only way to get promoted is to establish some kind of record for organizational athletics; to admit that we're overloaded is "chicken," to use the current adolescent term.

There is some very convincing research on the question of how living organisms cope with overload. James Miller and his colleagues in the Mental Health Research Institute of the University of Michigan have been doing some research on this problem, using all kinds of systems, from something as large as the Post Office at Christmastime to something as small as the dissected muscle of a frog.[2] They find that a limited number of concepts—ways of coping with overload—seems to be sufficient to describe what these systems do.

One such concept is *error*. As the organism gets overloaded, it begins to make mistakes. What also happens in cases of overload is *omission,* skipping things; and skipping things on an unorganized basis can be very dangerous living indeed in an organization.

Another way to cope with overload is *queuing*—that is, simply taking things in order. For example, you tell a role sender, "I've got a great deal to do. You see that stack? Well, the letter you sent is somewhere two-thirds of the way down, and when I get to it, you'll be answered." This is also living dangerously, because it doesn't take account of the relative power of the people who have created the queue or the importance of the issues, but some organizations get away with it. The Post Office, particularly at Christmastime, is a marvelous example of queuing, literally as well as in the figurative sense to which I refer here.

Slightly more sophisticated is the technique of *filtering*, making fast passes through the material and sorting things according to their relative importance, so that some things get through the filter and some don't. Incidentally, this method of coping with overload is the preferred solution in an exercise used in executive training courses. It is called the in-basket exercise, and presents each trainee with a large basket of material to go through (and make wise recommendations about) in a very limited period of time. It's interesting—and in a sense discouraging—to see the number of executives who will essentially queue; that is, go through the basket document by document, never getting beyond the middle or two-thirds of the way down before time is called, instead of filtering the papers into at least a few priority categories.

*Approximation* is another of the techniques that Miller has identified. "Approximation" means solving the problem of overload by

2. For a more complete description of this work, see James G. Miller, *Behavioral Science*, X (July, 1965), 193-237, and (October, 1965), 337-379 and 380-411.

simply doing a less careful job—relaxing the usual standards of accuracy or quality. The "quick and dirty" job is a colloquial and easily recognized label for approximation.

Finally, Miller mentions *escape,* which, by the way, we found to be one of the major responses to role conflict in our study. One can escape with dignity if he is high enough on the executive ladder— if he has a substantial suite of offices, a talented secretarial staff, a group of executive assistants, and a diversity of outside contacts and responsibilities so that travel is always appropriate and often required. A man who is locked into an assembly line with a short vacation and a limited budget, however, might have to do his escaping by fantasy rather than travel. The studies that have been done on the mental health of workers on repetitive jobs suggest they become all too good at fantasizing.

**Responses to Role Conflict**

When we talk about the focal person, we are concerned with two things on his part: what he thinks people want of him, and how he responds to it. His responses will be in part emotional, in part physiological, in part behavioral. Furthermore, his responses will reflect not only the objective facts of what the role set asks of him but also facts about his own personality, in interaction with their demands.

The distinction between a "real" conflict and a neurotic or inner, psychological conflict, which Dr. Zaleznik was talking about earlier this morning, comes into play here. In part, the conflict may be real, that is, it may exist in the overloading demands that the role set is making on the person; but any conflict will inevitably have some of the individual's personality in it. In extreme cases of hallucination or paranoid response, conflict is apparently *all* within the person and little or none in the immediate outside environment.

At any rate, we have discovered that the emotional costs of role conflict, in all its forms, are very predictable and very considerable. They include low job satisfaction, low confidence in the organization, and a high degree of job-related tension.

We find, as you would expect, that the more sensitive the person is the more exaggerated will be his responses to any given degree of conflict. We also find that the flexible personality may often be of more value to the organization than the rigid personality. The flexible person suffers more, but at the same time, paradoxically, the members of his role set are more satisfied with his responses. It is as if they were saying, "He may be suffering, but he is doing something about responding to our demands."

The rigid personality, in contrast, reports less experience of conflict when the objective situation is in fact conflict-ridden. He says in effect, "What conflict?" This may mean, of course, that he is responding in ways that would tend to manage or resolve the conflict from an organizational point of view. On the other hand, it may mean that he's staying in the kitchen, not so much because he can stand the heat as because he doesn't know it's hot. The response of the role set to the rigid person is to give up after a while. "There is no point in talking to so and so," or "What's the use of trying to get him to do such and such?" This can be costly for the organization, and in the long run, distressful for the person about whom we reach such con-

*Robert L. Kahn*

clusions. He runs the risk of being cast out for deficiencies he never recognized.

The single most frequent behavioral response to role conflict is withdrawal—escape or avoidance of the people who are seen as creating the conflict. This a particularly unhappy response from the organizational point of view, because it does something for the person using it at the expense of the organization. It does not essentially resolve or manage the conflict; it is therefore dysfunctional for the organization although it may be an act of self-preservation for the individual.

**Organizational Factors**

In any ongoing process, the focal person's behavior is observed by the members of his role set, and they in turn consider how they can influence him so that his future responses will be more in line with their expectations. If that were all, each little group of focal person and role set would spin on and on in organizational space, uninfluenced by anything else; but the organizational process is complicated by several factors that are persistently associated with the amount of objective conflict a person encounters.

These "organizational factors" have to do with the large structural facts of organizational life, which, in part, shape what the role set asks of the person. The members of the set are not just being whimsical in their demands; they are responding to some of the realities of their own organizational lives.

Three organizational factors directly concern us here. One of these is *size*. The bigger the organization, the more likely it is that people in it will report conflict. I am talking not about legal size, but about the size of that part of the organization in which a given person has membership.

Another factor is the *location* of the person's formal position in the organization. We find that the closer a person is to the boundary of the organization the more conflict he reports. A boundary person must meet expectations of people both inside and outside the organization. For example, if we ask a salesman to identify the members of his role set, some of them would be in the organization, and some of them (his customers) would be outside. The salesman's position is one of those in which conflict is created by people who have influence over him, but over whom he does not have reciprocal influence, or over whom he has influence only in very special or stylized ways.

The last of the organizational factors that tend to generate role conflict is *rank*. The higher the person is in the organization and the more people to whom he responds, both directly and indirectly, the more likely he is to report a large amount of role conflict—until we get to the very top of the organization. Somewhere between upper middle management and very top management, the curve of conflict seems not only to level off but to drop, which means either that the people who get to the top have remarkable tolerance for this kind of thing, or that something at the top echelons tends to ease the strain.

Finally, behavioral response to conflict is influenced by the background of interpersonal relations within the role set, and this background can be an asset or liability. We measured the amount of trust, liking, and respect that characterizes relationships within a role set, and we found that the greater the liking, trust, and respect the less distressful any given amount of objective conflict is likely to be. At the same time, the more consistent the conflict, the less likely it is that a large amount of trust, liking, and respect will continue to characterize those relationships. This suggests that the store of positive relationships within the role set is not inexhaustible. It is affected by what happens on a day-to-day basis; it can be spent and it can be renewed.

## Effects of Role Conflict on Productivity

These findings on role conflict came from a national survey and from a special study of 54 focal positions in a half-dozen companies. In more recent research, we have attempted to replicate these findings and determine to what extent they can predict productivity.[3] We have found, unexpectedly, that the amount of conflict a person experiences is related neither to his individual performance—except in extreme cases—nor to the performance of the organizational unit in which he operates. In other words, there is no tendency for harmonious organizational units to be the most productive. At least, this was so in one company where we compared approximately 150 units. Nor is the reverse tendency true. There are managers who say that "you have to keep the animals stirred up," "a little conflict does a lot for the muscle tone and the circulation of the red corpuscles," but we don't find this to be so.

The way in which conflicts are resolved, however, may permit a prediction of performance and productivity. We would predict a correlation between the use of the mutual resolution approach to conflict, and the judged satisfactoriness of the resolution and the subsequent performance. We would expect also that the major requirement for success in the mutual resolution method is the reciprocal influence of people in the role set.

## MANAGEMENT OF CONFLICT

I want now to discuss the question of conflict management in somewhat more detail by suggesting a few ideas on which I hope to be doing research, but for which I at present have no evidence except a collection of hunches—hunches about what we should pay attention to if we expect to be increasingly successful in conflict management and resolution.

### Time

One of the things we should pay attention to is *time*. That is, I think we can understand conflict better as a continuing process than as a momentary event. And I think the following aspects of time would be relevant to the question of conflict and the way it is handled: (1) When physicians talk about chronic illness, they talk about the *proportion of time in episode;* in other words, how much of the person's time is spent in the grip of illness? In our case, we could ask how much of the organization's time a particular unit spends in conflict. (2 What is the *duration of the episode?* How long does it take, in other words, to work through an episode of conflict? (3) What is the *interval between episodes?* How often and how regularly does the same conflict recur?

**3.** Allen I. Krant, Unpublished doctoral dissertation, University of Michigan, 1966.

## Space

A second dimension is that of *organizational space*. When conflict breaks out, how much of the organization becomes involved in it? I don't suggest that it is necessarily desirable to keep disagreements completely localized, but any given conflict has an appropriate domain, which would embrace positions that have some functional relationship to the issue being worked through. The pertinent questions would be: Has everyone who needs to get into this settlement been brought into it? Have we been able to avoid the miscellaneous onrush of people into the conflict just because it breaks the monotony?

## Form

A third broad issue that I would urge be considered in the management of conflict is simply the *form*. The Queensberry Rules have to do with conflict form, as do the rules of war. In organization, we take it for granted that physical conflict is out and that other forms are in—but what kinds? If I were charged with the responsibility of managing conflict in an organization, I would ask such questions as: Do rules exist for permissible forms of conflict? Are there norms? Do people in the organization agree as to what is permissible and what is not? To what extent do the permitted forms of conflict lead to resolution? Is the etiquette of conflict so constrained that permitted forms never allow for the real working through of the conflict? In other words, to what extent do we waltz through each round and leave without a blow having been struck, without any management having taken place?

These would be some of the questions that researchers might consider in the study of conflict, and that managers, since they can never wait for the researchers to catch up, might well consider in trying to make organization life more livable.

## HERBERT A. SHEPARD

*Visiting Professor, Yale School of Medicine, and Whittemore School of Business and Economics, University of New Hampshire.* Until 1966, Professor Shepard was Director of the Organizational Behavior Group, Case Institute of Technology. Earlier, he did organizational research and development work for Esso Standard Oil Company. In addition to teaching in administrative psychiatry and organizational behavior, he is consultant to a number of corporations and communities.

# INTEGRATING THE INDIVIDUAL
# INTO THE ORGANIZATION

The integration of the individual into the organization begins long before employment in one firm or another; it is my contention that this integration is partly accomplished by the schools, by the educational experiences of the child and the young adult. School systems have always asserted that they prepare students for life, and as I look at the curriculum of schools—elementary, high, and college—I find, in particular, that they train students to be good members of bureaucratic organizations. In the future I believe that this kind of educa-

89

tional experience will become increasingly less useful in meeting the needs of the society.

## The Educational Experience

To elaborate on this thesis, I have chosen the university as my example because it is the pinnacle of our culture, and, therefore, it should be a good place to find all of our ills in an advanced form.

In general, university people are well educated and work largely in isolation from one another, often at cross purposes. There is an emphasis on interpersonal and intergroup comparison and competition, both of which tend to push people away from competing against their own potential and toward trying to keep up with or outdo someone else. Furthermore, each person and each department has a high degree of territoriality. Each is constantly seeking new resources for his territory and protecting his own preserves against invasion. In short, in the academic world there is trained incapacity for collaborative activity and for building on others' resources. And it is these attitudes which form the implicit curriculum that is being passed on to our young people.

This structure of distrust (in which there is an attempt to control behavior in minute and detailed ways in order that no one may get away with anything) is one of the most impressive features of the university. One consequence of such an attitude is that the more psychopathic members of the institution expend their creativity in finding ways to beat the system, while the more conscientious expend their creativity in finding ways to adjust to it. Thus the system itself requires all the efforts that it was created to foster.

Another feature of the university is an impersonal and mechanical approach to others that demands repression of human feeling and denial of community, and tends to destroy the capacity for meaningful personal encounter. This impersonalism is accompanied by a relatively high degree of skill in handling conflict on a win-lose, compromise, or avoidance basis, and very little skill in inventive problem-solving to resolve a conflict. (Conflict resolution is distinguished from compromise in that after conflict resolution both sides emerge with something that neither foresaw and in that sense both sides win, while after compromise both sides forfeit something and thus are equally deprived.)

The features I have pointed out in the university can also be found in most companies, in most government agencies, and even in many families. In addition, these qualities—the emphasis on distrust and control, the isolation of the individual, and the incapacity for team-work—fit the needs of bureaucratic organizations extremely well. Students pick up these character traits, not because they are taught as part of the curriculum, but rather because they are part of the experience of school. Moreover, by depriving students of power and keeping them dependent while they are in school, we make them determined to achieve the things of which they have been deprived. Money and status in our culture are powerful rewards, and our school system does a good job of producing the kind of personality that seeks those rewards within the traditional organization structure.

**Patterns of Organization**

Our earliest industries were primarily manufacturing, and in order to efficiently produce goods on a regular schedule it was necessary to specify in detail what was to be done at each stage of production. Actually, what was needed was an automated factory; however, at that time we did not have the technological skills to create one. Consequently, where we might now use a non-living component, we used a living one and had to discover ways of making him behave as efficiently as a machine. To get the living component to do repeatedly a limited set of tasks, it was necessary to teach conformity and passivity and to overcome the human tendency to resist restriction and constriction of activity. The bureaucratic organizational system satisfied these requirements.

After the end of World War II, when the number of scientists and engineers began to increase and industry, government, and universities substantially increased their investments in research and development, it became apparent that scientists and engineers did not produce their best results within a bureaucratic organization. Consequently a search began for a way of organizing innovative activities that would work better than the traditional manufacturing or military methods.

Now, as both automation and research continue to increase, the problems of human interaction that previously occurred mostly in research departments will probably become characteristic of entire firms. This will necessitate the introduction and implementation of new organizational structures.

In fact, fairly recently several organizational forms have been developed that, in some ways, violate fundamental organizational principles of the past. These new forms have been given various labels: program management, matrix, and project and functional mix organizations. When these concepts were first introduced, they seemed to be only slight adjustments in bureaucratic theory. As they begin to mature, however, a number of old principles have to be discarded.

Program management, according to one interpretation, is a system for scheduling, budgeting, controlling and setting up accounts or programs. Although functionally arranged, the organization is to be responsive to project needs and therefore a group of program managers may be created to coordinate the various departments of an organization in carrying out the projects. Frequently, these people are little more than clerks and are subordinate in status to the functional heads of the department; they are not given enough stature to be influential or to really manage a program. They are dependent upon the cooperation of divisional managers, but, because of today's trained incapacity for teamwork, cooperation is something beyond the capabilities of most of the managers. Consequently, program or product or project management may be introduced but not make any significant difference in organization behavior or effectiveness.

An alternative interpretation of program management is that the organization formulates itself as a set of temporary programs of varying complexity. These programs have life cycles of varying duration; a set of permanent resources is established for accomplishing them. The problem then becomes how to use the organization's resources to do the diverse jobs of managing and carrying through multiple programs and, at the same time, ensure that the resources are used with maximum efficiency.

This kind or organization—also called a matrix organization—has two kinds of management people: functional managers who have particular sets of skills or resources under their command and who keep those resources in good shape, ready for action, and program managers who are charged with the responsibility for carrying out particular programs. Each program manager must rely on the resources of the functional managers; each functional manager must allocate resources to all programs, as needed. An advantage of the matrix organization is that the emphasis on program achievement tends to make the work more meaningful.

Is the matrix a possible and viable organizational form? At first glance, it appears to violate traditional principles: the program manager has a heavy responsibility for the completion of a program, yet he does not command the resources needed to fulfill his responsibility but must rely on the functional manager; similarly the functional manager is dependent upon the program manager for putting his resources to use but he is not responsible for how they are used. In other words, neither has authority in line with his responsibility.

Another problem is that unresolvable conflict at any level must be brought to the top of the organization for resolution because only the top man has matching authority and responsibility. When conflict occurs in the traditional organizational system, there is someone only one or two levels higher who can act as a Solomon and settle the disagreement. But in the matrix organization I have described, if people do not learn to resolve conflicts in some other way than by appealing to higher authority, Solomon will be hopelessly overloaded.

Despite these problems, program management is being used by older, well-established firms as well as those involved in advanced technology. To illustrate this increasing influence, one need only look at the tremendous impact on government agencies of the introduction by Johnson and McNamara of program management techniques. In one agency an executive, by a stroke of the pen, removed four levels of organization—something that is most unusual in government bureaucracies. He also made programs the means of control and had fifty people reporting directly to him.

**Education for Teamwork**

Now that we have examined both the traditional bureaucratic system and the new matrix system, I want to discuss the integration of the individual into the various organizational forms. A matrix organization in effect creates the need for teamwork—a new requirement for organizations—not only across interpersonal lines, but also across intergroup lines. It requires that individuals be effective members of several teams simultaneously. It forces almost every person in the organization to be responsive to several people, not just to a single boss; it also reduces the degree to which anyone can feel like a boss.

These are such radical changes that a new problem arises: how do we educate people to participate in such a system, or, perhaps more realistically, how can we educate college students to prepare them for such a system? Let me answer by describing an experiment done at Case a few years ago with a sophomore introductory course in dynamic analysis. A course council, consisting of the professor, instructors, and student-chosen representatives, served as a feed-back link between the leaders of the course and the students and was also involved in much of the planning for the course, including methods of evaluation, examinations, and pace. The professor lectured once a week and set the examinations. This enabled the instructors to serve as consultants and advisors rather than evaluators. The students were divided into teams of five or six. Many of the homework problems were formulated in such a way that they were best solved by the team. Each team was given a miniaturized computer so that a piece of equipment further bound them together. The group was also given an hour each week in which they could meet with one of the instructors for consultation on their homework problems. The short time allotted was another means of forcing the group to work together to complete as much of the homework as possible before they met with the instructor.

These changes made quite a difference in the atmosphere of the class, and the students did learn something about teamwork. After completing their four years at Case, the participants were asked to rate all of their courses. This introductory course received high ratings in all areas and particularly in the learning of concepts. These ratings are especially enlightening when one considers that there was actually less lecturing and formal presentation of concepts than in most other courses. In the process of working together and teaching each other, the students gained greater insight into the phenomena and principles with which they were concerned.

This experiment is the exception. It is generally forbidden for students to help each other; this is called copying or cheating. The student is supposed to operate on his own and is graded on his individual efforts. Thus, the experience of education, at least currently, restricts the growth of the capacity for teamwork and adaptability.

## Conclusion

The educational system is not going to change suddenly because of a few people within it. By and large, the schools are the way they are because of what those outside the schools are demanding of them. Moreover, although for business firms the potential payoff of new organization structures, working relationships, and decision-making processes is worth the risk of experimentation, to school systems it is often unclear where there is any payoff for experimentation. The innovative educator can be certain, however, that no matter what he tries, he will be criticized either by other educators or by the community.

Thus we are faced with a situation in which a young person finishes school with skills, attitudes, and values that are in accord with the traditional style of organization. If more complex, organic work structures are to be successfully implemented, each child will need school experiences that go beyond mere talk of working with other people and that actually include ways of and practice in working with them. It is only when the community really wants these attitudes and values instilled in its children, however, that the schools will be forced to experiment with the learning climates, methods, and relationships that will foster them.

**HARVEY SHERMAN**

*Director, Organization and Procedures Department, the Port of New York Authority.* Mr. Sherman has served as public administration advisor for the Near East, Africa, and South Asia, U. S. Foreign Operations Administration, and as director, public administration staff, U. S. Technical Corporation Administration; he has also held several positions in the United States Bureau of the Budget. Mr. Sherman has taught management and public administration courses at Syracuse University, at the United States Department of Agriculture Graduate School, and at City College of New York.

# A PRAGMATIC APPROACH TO ORGANIZATION

During the recession in 1949, Sears, Roebuck and Company made a study of the organization of its intermediate-sized stores. It showed that with no directives from headquarters two basic patterns had developed: one, which I shall call type X, would have a manager (and sometimes an assistant manager) to whom some 32 departments reported directly; the other, which I shall call type Y, would have a manager and five or six assistant managers, each of whom would have five or six departments reporting to him.

In analyzing these two types of organization on the bases of profit, cost, and promotable people, Sears, Roebuck found that type X was clearly more effective on all measures. Further analysis showed the reasons. The type X manager tended to select department heads whom he believed could do the job. He gave them responsibility and then let them alone. If a man couldn't do the job, he was replaced.

Under the type Y system, however, if a department head was weak, the assistant manager would often step in and nearly run the department for him. The assistant manager was constantly looking over his subordinates' shoulders. (Incidentally, type X managers tended to be optimists, believing that if you let people alone they would do a good job. Type Y managers tended to be pessimists; they thought people were no good and had to be watched all the time. They often used expressions like "What's happened to this modern generation?" and "People are not what they used to be.")

Sears, Roebuck did some experimenting by shifting managers. They took a type X manager and put him in charge of a type Y store; he soon decided to save money by eliminating the intermediate level of managers. When the company put a type Y manager in charge of a type X store, he quickly decided he needed assistance to supervise his people and established an intermediate level.

**Situational Problem-Solving**

I am not trying to say that a large span of control is always better than a small one, to use the jargon of organization. But for the intermediate-sized Sears, Roebuck store, in 1949, the large span of control was more effective than the small. This might not be true for other companies or for Sears, Roebuck at other times or even for the company's larger or smaller stores. In other words, the point of the story is that organization problems—and undoubtedly other management problems—are situational. Although there may be some likenesses among different enterprises, the practicing manager doesn't deal in generalizations, but must solve a given problem at a given time, in a given place, in a given culture, and with given people.

Actually, it seems to me to be more valuable to talk about "organizing," rather than "organization," problems because, unfortunately, the word "organization" has come to mean the company itself, and that is not my subject. I define "organizing" as the process of grouping activities and responsibilities and of establishing formal and informal relationships that will enable people to work together most effectively in determining and accomplishing the objectives of an enterprise. That is a fairly long definition. A shorter one is simply "dividing up the work."

For a specific example, here is a relatively simple kind of organizing problem that has been presented to me many times. Department XYZ has two branches, A and B, and each branch has two sections. The head of branch A has left the organization and the head of department XYZ calls me in for advice: should he fill this job and continue the same organization, or should he abolish the position and raise the sections of A to branch level where they would be reporting directly to him?

I challenge anyone to tell me one accepted principle of organization that would help solve this relatively simple problem. There are certain mechanical considerations, of course, such as how much money would be saved if the job wasn't filled (incidentally, in many cases we find that it would cost money rather than save it if the job weren't filled). Another such question would be how the sections of branch A compare with branch B in terms of budget, size of staff, and importance of function. But the really important factors are more personal. For example, what is the caliber of the two men who head the sections of A? Are they both senior, competent, able people who can operate at the higher level? Is one of them very good and the other not so good, in which case the better one would expect, and should be given, a promotion to the vacant position? How would the head of B react if the section heads were raised to his level? How would the section heads in branch B react if their counterparts in branch A were promoted?

These are the considerations that should be, and are, taken into account in solving such a problem, and all the usually mentioned principles of organization, such as putting related functions together, or making sure that everyone reports to only one boss, have little or no relevance to the solution.

Let me further illustrate my point by a slightly more complex organizing problem that occurred at the Port Authority.

In 1962, through legislation in the states of New York and New Jersey, the Port of New York Authority was required to take over the then bankrupt Hudson and Manhattan commuter railroad. New Yorkers sometimes refer to this facility as the Hudson Tubes, but we at the Port Authority know it as PATH, Port Authority Trans-Hudson Railroad. Taking over the railroad presented an organizing problem that appeared to have three basic solutions: we could contract for the running of PATH; we could make it a regular line or operating department within the Port Authority, either as a new department or under an existing department; or we could set PATH up as a subsidiary corporation. We chose the last alternative. What led us to this conclusion?

We decided not to use an agent under contract because, first, we couldn't find a contractor that we considered qualified; second, using a contractor would make it hard to apply Port Authority standards to the operation of PATH; third, if we used an agent it might appear to the public that we were avoiding the responsibility given us by the legislatures; and fourth, we thought the Port Authority would miss an exciting challenge if we ran PATH by contract. We wanted to see if we could run a railway effectively.

We didn't give PATH to one of our existing departments or set up a new line department because it was very difficult to assimilate the Hudson and Manhattan staffs. For one thing, the Hudson and Manhattan had twelve unions. These were typical railroad unions, organizations that were different from the unions we were used to in the Port Authority. Another problem was that the Hudson and Manhattan staffs came under a different retirement system and different labor laws. In addition, the railroad was under the very strict control of the Interstate Commerce Commission. If we set it up as a regular part of the Port Authority, the Interstate Commerce Commission might want to review all our books and could become involved in our other operations; we wanted to isolate the Hudson and Manhattan enough to confine ICC control to that particular area.

The result of this reasoning was that we set up the railroad as a subsidiary corporation, so that it could continue its operations with the existing Hudson and Manhattan staffs while we in the Port Authority learned how to run a railroad. Port Authority management philosophy was brought to bear on the railroad, but the subsidiary was separate as far as unions, retirement, etc., were concerned, and ICC regulation was confined to the subsidiary corporation.

The next problem was where to assign the new subsidiary. We could put it under an existing line department, we could create a new line department to supervise it, or we could have it report directly to our executive director (a position equivalent to the presidency of a private company). We eliminated the possibility of giving PATH to an existing line department because all of them were already burdened with their own operations and we didn't think any of the directors had the time, energy, or knowledge to take on this additional load. We didn't have PATH report directly to the executive director because the many new policy problems involved would take too much of his time. We thought we needed a new department director, equivalent to a vice president, who could be concerned entirely with the railroad's problems, so we decided to set up a new line department, which we called the Rail Transportation Department.

The third problem was what to do with the relationships between the existing Hudson and Manhattan staff units (law, personnel, finance, etc.) and the Port Authority staff units. Here again, there were three general possibilities. We could consolidate Hudson and Manhattan and Port Authority staff units; we could keep them separate; or we could keep the Hudson and Manhattan staff units decentralized but have them report to their counterparts in the Port Authority. Here, we didn't use one solution for all units. We consolidated the lawyers, the other Hudson and Manhattan staff units stayed at their own headquarters but reported to the corresponding units in the Port Authority.

This is a familiar Port Authority pattern for operations, but it had additional value here because the top Hudson and Manhattan staff had gone with the trustee into bankruptcy. They had formed a sort of paper organization that was involved in a long court battle with the Port Authority concerning how we would pay for the railroad. Thus the top staff was no longer a part of the organization, so it was necessary for the remaining staff to report to someone who could supervise the operation.

Here was an organizing problem, and the solutions we worked out were unique and dependent upon the particular situation. In the process of making these decisions, I can't remember that we ever mentioned any of the usual organization principles, although it is possible we had them subconsciously in mind. In other words, what worked for us and what I am recommending is a pragmatic approach to organization problems: doing what works, with due regard for both the short- and long-range objectives.

**Principles of Organization**

Now let me turn my attention to the problem of organization principles. As Herb Simon has pointed out, principles of organization are very much like proverbs in that they frequently contradict each other. For example, "Look before you leap," but "He who hesitates is lost." What do we do too often in the field of organization is make a decision and then pick the principle that supports it.

In some of the earlier discussions the question was raised whether or not planning should be separated from operations. This is a good example of the conflict of principles. One principle says that if the planning and operations are carried out together, the immediate problems involved in operations will prevent the planning from getting done. But another principle says that if you separate operations from planning, planning is done in a vacuum and is not realistic.

Almost any accepted principle of organization can be shown to be unworkable under some circumstances. For instance, let's look at the principle that every man should have one boss. More often than not, this isn't the case. A secretary may work for more than one person, and a president may report to his company's board of directors; each has more than one boss. A ship commander in the Navy takes orders from the group commander on how to run his ship and from the fleet commander on where to run it. In my own department of organization and procedures (which in industry would be equivalent to a combination of organization planning, and systems and procedures) my title is director, and I have a deputy director. The department is organized into a sort of pool from which people are assigned to projects as they come up. Project 1 may be handled by senior management analyst A, assisted by junior management analyst B. Project 2 may be handled by senior management analyst C, assisted by junior management analyst B. Then junior management analyst B may be doing project 3 on his own. Even in this oversimplified version you can see that junior management analyst B has at least four bosses: on the first project, senior management analyst A; on the second, senior management analyst C; and on the third, both the deputy director and me.

Does this cause problems? Of course. One man is played off against another, everyone fights for analyst B's time, etc. Yet for our purposes, the advantages of our system far outweigh the disadvantages.

## Prospects for Organization

Now let me look ahead. Some things I think will have an important effect on the organization of the future are size, the changing composition of the work force, the change in business-government relationships as it becomes harder and harder to draw a line between what's business and what's government, and technological and scientific developments in the management area.

But far more important than any of these factors is the rate of technological change. Bruce Henderson, vice president of Arthur D. Little, has said, "The most significant fact of our times, overshadowing all else, is the tremendous rate of change that we are experiencing." I can see seven major developments growing out of this rapid rate of change.

First, top management will have to recognize its responsibility for establishing a climate in which changes in organizaton are accepted and welcomed; the emphasis must shift from stability, formality, and orthodoxy toward flexibility, informality, and more, not fewer intuitive decisions.

Second, I think the objectives of an enterprise will have to be less rigidly defined, because prompt revisions in objectives will be necessary to meet changes in environment and technology.

Third, definitions of responsibility will have to be less rigid. A job description should not describe a job as it is now, but should be worded to permit the man on the job to undertake anything new comes up that he is capable of handling. Similarly, there should be much less emphasis on requiring specific experience for a job and more stress on the person's flexibility, adaptability, inventiveness, and ability to grow.

Fourth, there will be a need to adjust the widely accepted equilibrium model of organization. This model puts too much emphasis on stability and treats change as an episodic phenomenon. Moreover, it assumes that equilibrium is an end in itself rather than a means for achieving such objectives as productivity and profit. A new model is needed that recognizes change as a continuing process— that sees an organization as constantly changing, rather than reaching set stages of equilibrium between periods of change. The model must also recognize that the ambiguity and uncertainty that often result from change are not necessarily bad.

Fifth, there will be more frequent use of the task force approach instead of the usual hierarchical structure. Teams will be drawn from various parts of the enterprise for specific tasks or projects and the members returned to their units or assigned to new projects as each task is completed.

Sixth, more emphasis will be given to long-range planning, and to study of the external environment and the effect that changes in that environment have on the policy of management and the organization of an enterprise.

And seventh, there will be more instances of the establishment of a special organization unit whose job will be to question everything, including the objectives of the enterprise. There will be, in effect, a vice president for revolution.

## JOSEPH H. McPHERSON

*Manager of Personnel Research and Development, Dow Chemical Company.* Before assuming his present position, Dr. McPherson served as manager of the Dow Psychology Department for thirteen years. He has conducted four "creativity experiences" (with Hollis Peter, L. C. Repucci, and S. A. Gregory) for the Foundation for Research on Human Behavior, Ann Arbor, Michigan. He also participated in four of the five University of Utah Conferences on Identification of Creative Scientific Talent.

# THE SMALL GROUP, THE ORGANIZATION, AND THE CREATIVITY DOMAIN

I want to begin with a series of provocative questions: What good does it do for us to hire strong people, people with the ego, the independence, the aggressiveness that we need for creativity, if we don't keep them strong by motivating them according to their individual dispositions? What good does it do to hire strong people and then place them in groups that have among their goals reducing strong men to passivity? What good does it do to hire strong people and place them in strong groups if their energies will then be devoted to warring with other groups within the organization? What good does it do to hire strong people and place them in strong groups that are unified in their objectives if the organization itself is narrow in

111

its objectives, inflexible, conflict-ridden at the top, and lacks a program for self-renewal? To go one step further, what good does it do to have strong people, strong groups, and a strong, cohesive organization with a program for self-renewal if the organization doesn't have any money or any resources to sustain it? And how can any of these problems be solved if the doctors, the organizational specialists like you and me, are so limited in their scope and so plagued with their own domain problems and status struggles that their prescriptions for the organization look tainted to their patients?

These questions led me to four objectives for this presentation:

1. To relate small group variables and organizational variables to each other and to the creativity domain.
2. To indicate the nature of current training and research in the small group area.
3. To indicate the nature of the work being done at the organizational level.
4. To look at some of the problems of integrating the findings of these diverse fields into a comprehensive program.

**The Creativity Domain**

I use the term "creativity domain" to connote all the creative aspects of an individual and all the variables that may affect his creativity. Managers, particularly those who have industrial relations functions, must concern themselves with all aspects of the domain. They must understand the intellectual and emotional characteristics of the creative person. They must understand the methods by which he is

Joseph H. McPherson

selected (the research done at the University of Utah[1] will help here). They must understand his various problem-solving and creative processes and how these processes relate to his individual personality. They also ought to explore how various physiological processes relate to creativity (a field where we lack knowledge) and how education can enhance the creativity of people. It is also necessary to understand the possible effects of the positive and negative aspects of other persons, especially members of the work group or the immediate manager. Situational variables like crises or good times can influence creativity, as can management's own policies and procedures. All these aspects of creativity must be explored simultaneously if the domain itself is to be understood.

At Dow I had an opportunity, working with a group of scientists, to trace the steps in the development of some inventions within the company. We isolated the major variables that seemed to be involved, and developed a symbolic language to show the interaction between these variables. The result was the "Dynamics of Invention" exhibit, now lodged in one of our large buildings. By means of sound and lighted symbols, this 15-minute exhibit illustrates the interaction between strong persons and weak persons, between people who recognize and meet needs and people who do not, between people who communicate their results and people who cannot. It interrelates the effects of strong groups, weak groups, obstacles, and management decisions. It integrates the short-range concerns of patents, products, procedures, papers, reputation, morale, and money with the long-

1. See Calvin Taylor, ed., *Creativity: Progress and Potential* (New York: McGraw-Hill, 1964); Calvin Taylor and Frank Barron, eds., *Scientific Creativity: Its Recognition and Development* [Selected Papers from the Proceedings of the First, Second, and Third University of Utah Conferences: "The Identification of Creative Scientific Talent"] supported by the Natonal Science Foundation (New York: Wiley, 1963).

range concerns of expansion, continuity, diversification, renewal, and meaning and purpose for employees.

The exhibit has been useful in teaching our young people about some of the difficulties of introducing a new invention in industry, particularly in giving them some idea of the time involved. It also fits in with our need to portray the contributions of many of our functions (including the classical ones of marketing, production, engineering, and development), those small creative groups that cause an idea to progress from initial formulation to money.

Now let me turn to the subject of small group and organizational variables. Small group variables are defined as those operating within a person's immediate work group. Organizational variables involve the methods whereby small groups are knitted into a large organization as well as the management of the organization, its policies and decision-making methods, etc. I shall begin with the small group.

**Research in Small Groups**

For years Dow has been offering managers an opportunity to participate in a training experience called Management Training II or sensitivity training. This program is similar to the National Training Laboratories program. Each training group is composed of approximately fourteen managers from different parts of the organization. Before a manager enters the program, members of his work group describe him, using an adjective check list I developed. They also describe their group, using an instrument developed by me but much influenced by R. Likert.[2] The manager ultimately receives information from both lists. Approximately two-thirds of the one week's training time is spent in unstructured group situations and the other one-third is devoted to discussing theories of group growth and development, leadership styles, membership roles, and similar topics.

Since the program's inception 19 trainers have worked with about 100 of these training groups. We have done a considerable amount of research with the instruments, and now have normative data for approximately 615 work groups representing 4,000 subordinates. Results show that the descriptions provided by the instruments reflect quite accurately the subjective observations of members and management, and thus suggest that a manager can use the instruments to compare his group to other groups in the company. The results have also drawn our attention to such differences as that between the manager's perception of the group and the group's own views, and those between the perceptions of marketing, production, and research and development units. Another interesting, although perhaps not surprising, tendency which we noted is that managers tend to evaluate the "upward" group to which they belong (where their boss is the appointed leader and they are the subordinates) as less effective than their own groups.

We also did factor analytic studies of the results to see if we could discover a more economical set of factors to describe group life. The four that seem most important are cohesion, faith in the environment, achievement orientation, and autonomy.

A different part of the study used another instrument (adapted from one developed by Dr. Seymour Levy of Pillsbury Flour), to assess the managers' relative orientation toward McGregor's Theory X and

**2.** Both instruments appear in J. H. McPherson, *The Creative Manager* (Midland, Michigan: Hawkins Publishing Company, 1965). See also R. Likert, *New Patterns of Management* (New York: McGraw-Hill, 1961).

Theory Y. As you know, McGregor used the terms Theory X and Theory Y to describe two attitudes which management may have toward employees. Theory X holds that employees need firm and relatively constant direction. Theory Y, in contrast, holds that only self-motivated employees are creative and implies, therefore, that management should direct its attention to the nature of the needs of employees and how to appeal to these needs.

Sensitivity training, as developed by the National Training Laboratories, is directly related to Theory Y. In these sessions (often called "T" groups) men are encouraged to state openly their attitudes and feelings toward other members of the group and the nature of the group itself. The hope is that after listening to other participants each man will be more sensitive to interpersonal relationships and will use this sensitivity in determining others' motivational needs. We found that sensitivity training changed participants' assumptions about people and moved them more in the direction of Theory Y. The training also helped them to see their groups as the groups saw themselves. We also found that members of a trained manager's work group observed a change toward group goal setting (an aim of sensitivity training) in their manager. In addition they themselves felt more achievement-oriented, saw more clearly that they had a good future, and tended to see their work as exciting and rewarding.

**Organizational Studies**
The third objective of this paper is to look at the nature of the current training and research being done at the organizational level. Dow has instituted product management teams composed of representatives

from the basic functions (marketing, production, and research and development). Such a team is responsible for all aspects of developing and marketing a particular product and must therefore influence persons and groups in the organization over whom they have no actual control.

John Vail of our corporate education department and Jay Lorsh of the Harvard Business School have been studying the operation of our teams to discover what kind of interaction within these teams is most productive. They find that each function has a different and characteristic view of the departmental structure it needs (e.g., production thinks it needs quite a bit of structure, marketing believes it needs a minimal amount); time requirements (particularly in extended periods); orientation toward each other (e.g., marketing tends to take a more personal approach); and the environment. The findings suggest that these differences may be useful rather than detrimental and that the ways in which team members integrate their efforts and resolve their conflicts differentiate the successful teams from the unsuccessful ones.

## Integrating the Findings

The last objective of this paper is to present some of the problems of integrating these various findings so that they will be more useful in the future. First let me stress the need to relate the organizational variables and small group variables to styles of leadership and to task and situation variables. The conditions (both of task and situation) that lead to excesses in communication, integration, and cohesion must be explored as thoroughly as deficiences in these areas.

The relationship between an interlocking system of plans and small group and organizational variables must be developed. Strategic plans (25 years), corporate development plans, diversification plans, divestment plans—all the plans in the system—need to be related to various aspects of human personality, to small group variables, and the interrelationships between the two. In addition, multiple sets of variables for measuring performance are made necessary by the variations among the tasks performed by such varied groups as accounting, economic evaluation and fundamental research. Some of the criteria that I think might be included, as appropriate, are achievement of the profit plan, achievement of the cost reduction goals, anticipation of difficulties and making the necessary changes, flexibility of the group when changes are required, cooperation with neighboring groups of the organization, contribution to the success of some of these other groups, innovations in the product line, and innovations that ensure continuity of the organization.

The final problem I must cite involves sensitivity training and the need for openness, trust, and conflict resolution, which are emphasized in such training. These values must be reexamined in the context of social power to see if they will help or hurt the person who believes in them. What degree of openness, for example, is appropriate in a group where the search for power is ruthless? Do openness and trust have value if the total system is not open or if the trainee is not equipped with some insights about how to survive in a closed system?

Thus, as you can see, we still have much to learn. I hope that these initial efforts will help to spur progress across this vital field.

**FRANK J. JASINSKI**

*Director of Career Development, TRW Systems Group.* Prior to joining the TRW Systems Group, Dr. Jasinski taught at the Yale Schools of Engineering and of Medicine and did organizational research for business and industry. At present, he is concerned with organizational improvement, including managerial and technical development and optimal utilization of professional, technical, and support personnel. Mr. Jasinski is also involved in a study of the leadership function in team development, of resolving intergroup conflict, and of organizational change.

120

## DEALING WITH GROUP CONFLICT—
## A PROBLEM-CENTERED APPROACH

I would like to avoid further emphasizing the distinction between practitioners and theoreticians, and instead explore a middle road by focusing on problems and problem-solving. In this context, conflict within a group is not always a bad thing; in fact, it can be a source of constructive energy.

First, I would like to talk about the nature of group conflict, at least as we have experienced it and used it; second, about the behavioral and nonbehavioral approaches to conflict; and third, about working with a problem. Finally, I would like to talk about the team development process we have used at TRW Systems.

121

*Frank J. Jasinski*

## Nature of Group Conflict

Group conflict can occur in a variety of contexts: within an established work group that is to continue as a group; between groups that are interdependent and have to work together to get a joint task accomplished; within a newly created work group, where conflict exists almost by definition; and in reconfigured groups, where an existing group is reorganized or two or more groups are brought together or separated. Still another kind of group conflict occurs when, for instance, a service function loses touch with the real business of the company.

Let us begin by recognizing that a group must cope with its environment, just as an individual must. When a group is unable to cope with its task, its surroundings, itself, or other groups, it is in conflict. A group in conflict can have a negative effect on decision-making in at least two ways: (1) it can provide insufficient or erroneous data for decision-making, or (2) it can limit the range of decisions by its inability to cope with decisions beyond certain limits.

Let me turn now to the ongoing work group. Difficulties can emerge here for a variety of reasons. One cause can be a change in personnel; another, a change in the environment in which the group had been comfortably adjusted. Another problem can be the building-up of emotional debris—where the minor, day-to-day irritations within the group accumulate and produce real conflict.

Examples of such problems can be drawn from a training group that I once managed. At one point we began adding a number of new professionals and support personnel. At the same time a new role was emerging for the group: previously we had been fairly centralized, but now we were working more and more toward decentralization. Thus the group had changed and was changing, but no one outside the group recognized this fact. Capable new people were coming in from different backgrounds, each bringing his own repertoire of roles. The new people were not as effective as they might have been because they did not know what the new environment was and could not adapt to it. When they tried to find out about the group so that they could adapt, the information they collected was more like mythology and folklore—it was about a group which existed two or three years in the past. Their use of this garbled data to establish their behavior caused a considerable amount of difficulty, especially at the level of emotional debris. And, as a further complication, when they didn't know what else to do, they naturally tended to fall back into the roles that had been effective in their former environments. It took an extended session devoted to these problems to enable the group to begin to function well as a unit.

The second context for group conflict that I mentioned was that of interdependent groups. These situations become very difficult to deal with because it is so hard to separate the symptoms of conflict from the causes. For example, is a breakdown of communications a cause of conflict or a symptom that conflict already exists?

Let us consider two interdependent groups who had to compete for scarce resources, and whose needs were equally pressing. This case involved a computer; together the groups required at least 28

*Frank J. Jasinski*

hours of computer time per day. A lot of emotional debris resulted from the constant jockeying to get "more than a fair share" of machine time, dollars, and manpower. On top of this, one group was made up of programmers, the other of operators, and they had difficulty in talking to each other because they were working from different frames of reference. Soon they weren't talking to each other at all, because each group had made its own assessment of the situation, based on its own experience and its own discipline. In addition, partly because the groups reported to different vice presidents, they had no viable organizational mechanism through which to work out these differences.

A third situation in which conflict can emerge is the creation of a new work group. People are brought together who don't know who is going to do what or who is responsible for what. They know that the interdependency vital to any group must be established, but they are unclear where to start, where to intermesh. They are also faced with the lack of adequate interpersonal knowledge: how are other members going to interact or respond to various kinds of stimuli?

A fourth situation of group conflict results from the reconfiguration of work groups. Job responsibilities or relationships may be changed without the knowledge of some members of the group. Then one day someone says, "We are doing things differently now." The uninformed group member may have had a lot of loyalty to his particular group, but that is submerged by another loyalty, loyalty to self. He feels insecure because he doesn't know where he stands or who is going to measure him and how.

124

The problem becomes worse when two or more groups are merged. I once worked with a group that was the result of a merger of three. There were three separate sets of loyalties. Each group felt a certain sense of failure because they had been forced together without any say in the decision. Individuals felt they had lost status— former managers, for instance, were no longer managers. The combined groups had a new boss whom they didn't know and with whom they no idea how to deal. Then the market slumped a little, causing a decrease in the growth rate of each group's functions. Thus we had a situation where roles were outdated and people were called on to develop new loyalties to an organization they didn't really understand or appreciate. The resultant attitudes of group members were, as could be expected, poor. Some were defensive and others refused to go along with the new state of affairs.

The last kind of group conflict that I mentioned involves a disconnected or disoriented group—for example, a service function that over a period of time has lost touch with the rest of the organization. It continues to provide what it regards as adequate and appropriate services, but either the requirements of the company have changed or other groups' perception of the service function has changed. The service function knows only that its performance is unsatisfactory. Its usual response is to give more of the same kind of service—which was inadequate in the first place and now, in larger volume, is even less satisfactory. The result is alienation between the service group and the organization (which often starts developing its own resources and ignores the service group). This separation may also be accentuated by legalistic processes, such as getting the president of the company to sign new regulations (so that his agreement can be used as an argument). The relationship between the service group and the organization tends to become very legalistic and argumentative and definitely unproductive. Criticism of this state of affairs only elicits defensiveness and greater reliance on standard operating procedures.

**Two Theoretical Approaches**

These, then, are some of the kinds of group conflicts that occur and with which I have worked. Now we come to talk of possible solutions for group conflict. The large variety that have been applied derive from a number of different theoretical bases. For ease of understanding, however, let us oversimplify and divide the theoreticians into two classes, nonbehavioral and behavioral. In the nonbehavioral class I would include the classic mechanistic and scientific people— I might call them the scientific management group. They are concerned with distinguishing and clarifying the overall needs of the organization (as are the operations research people, who are more mathematically oriented and do the same thing using slide-rules and formulas).

The advantage of the nonbehavioral approach is that its solutions tend to make responsibilities clear. They deal specifically with what is required and who is expected to do it. Even interdependencies are written down and established. These interdependencies tend to be established in work and organizational terms, a valid approach because work flow and organization can be specified quite precisely.

126

And when they are reduced to writing, everyone presumably understands them.

Such written evaluations and outlines are particularly helpful when we are dealing with interdependent groups, especially if they have undergone reconfiguration but are tending to fall back on precedent. This approach is also useful in dealing with a disconnected or disoriented group. In both cases the nonbehaviorists say, "Here are the rules, here's the way you better do it."

A real problem lies in the fact that the nonbehavioral theoreticians assume that the environment is relatively stable and that it doesn't change over time. They assume that it is possible to describe all cases, all possibilities, all variables. They also make assumptions about the rationality of man. They think that if a man reads their directives and evaluations, he will understand their logic and will do as he is told. They tend also to assume that the task or the organization is paramount, that this is what an employee is being paid for and that he can either be fitted to a job or replaced.

In contrast, the solutions that derive from the behavioral approach stress the necessity of understanding a man's needs; they say you must motivate a man by satisfying his needs. They recommend that you facilitate the relationships between men and that you allow for variations and individuality.

We attempted to use this second approach in the group I mentioned earlier, the one that had been joined by a number of new people. We tried to get to know each other and to adapt to each other on the basis of mutual commitment and trust.

*Frank J. Jasinski*

But none of this worked. Why? I would suggest that one reason is the assumption made by those subscribing to the behavioral science approach that there is an innate conflict between the organization and the individual. They seem to assume that it is impossible for both the organization and the individual to come out on top. They believe that the conflict can only be resolved by some kind of compromise or by one losing to the other. The behavioral approach also assumes that the man-to-man relationship is overridingly important (and hence that the task of the organization is secondary). Here again we are getting into the whole syndrome of the organization versus the individual, the assumption that a man has to be motivated on his own terms and its corollary, that his terms differ from organizational terms.

**Working the Problem**

We have looked at the advantages and disadvantages of both the nonbehavioral and the behavioral approaches when they are applied to particular situations, and neither seems to work as well as its proponents would like. Now let me suggest that in each case the fundamental problem has been the tendency to concentrate too much on theory, and hence to use one approach or one solution to the exclusion of all others.

Therefore let me recommend that we forget about theory and approaches and focus on the problem or set of problems. When we do this, I believe we will help the group or groups deal more effectively with their conflicts.

I like to use the illustration of the operating room to show the advantage of focusing on the problem. If you were to watch an operating team that had worked together for a time and had done a particular operation several times before, you would notice that they can do an hour or hour-and-a-half operation without saying a single word. Everybody seems to know what to do at the right time. If you were an interactionist, you would say that the head nurse is the person who initiates action for the team, because she is the one who picks instruments up and puts them into the surgeon's hand. But this evaluation is not valid—what runs the group is the condition of the patient. Each member of the team recognizes this and knows what he is supposed to do with respect to each change in the patient's condition.

At TRW Systems we try to help groups attain this same kind of focus, this problem-centered approach. Our development process aims to help groups become more effective and more able to cope with their problems by first identifying the problems, then exploring alternative solutions, and finally selecting and using the best alternative. We blend whatever approaches are needed, whether they are technical, organizational, interpersonal, or personal. The important thing is the condition of the patient, the problem. We build around the problem; we don't make the problem or people fit into preexisting situations.

**Team Development at TRW**

Since 1964, TRW has sharply increased its emphasis on team development, a process in which groups ask themselves what they as groups needed to do to become more effective. Members are also asked if an extended staff meeting would help, and if so, in what way. The number of meetings increased ten-fold in 1965, and dou-

129

bled again in each of the next two years. These problem-centered meetings obviously worked. Managers experience them, and get things accomplished.

To show you how and why they work, let me describe in some detail a meeting on one of our spacecraft programs and then summarize our experience with what we think are the essential characteristics of the team development process.

We were in a competition in which two of the three participants would be eliminated; we had about 12 weeks to prepare a study proposal. This would require about 24 people, six of whom had been in on the initial proposal; the other 18 were almost completely unknown to each other. We decided on a two-day meeting, which would also include three people from another company, a major subcontractor. Before the meeting, I interviewed the managers of several groups, asking, "What do you think this group needs to be effective, to get the study done on time and well done?" The answers served as the initial agenda for the meeting. The central issue was "What do we need to do as a group when the proposal request comes in?"

Since many of the workers didn't even know what the bosses looked like, we began by using a fishbowl technique. The six managers and one of the subcontractor's men sat in the center of the room and the remainder of the people sat on the outskirts and watched these seven discuss the initial agenda. They saw how the leaders perceived the agenda and how they responded to it and to each other. After two hours, the meeting was opened to a half-hour of comments and questions from the rest of the group. The end

130

result was a modification of the original agenda into a list of problems that had to be resolved.

The next morning we broke into small, function-oriented groups. In some cases these groups were meeting for the first time; they had never had a staff meeting before. These meetings were for the group members to get to know each other and to identify the problems they anticipated having with other groups.

That afternoon and evening we began combining: group one met with group four, group two with group three; then on the next round group one met with group two, etc. After each group had a chance to work with every other group, we identified another set of problem areas. Because some problems involved three groups instead of just two, the next morning and early afternoon were spent in problem-oriented groups. These cut across work groups to deal with individual, specific problems.

Did it work? After two days the head of the contingent from the other company said, "I didn't want to come. When I first heard about being invited, I was scared to death....When I finally convinced myself my job depended on it, I decided to come. I must tell you, I never felt closer to a work group in my whole work history than I do to this particular group. In fact, I am going back and tell my management; this is the only way to deal with subcontractors."

Not only were the participants greatly impressed by the meeting, the groups formed were so cohesive that when we had to hire several new men two weeks later, they had difficulty breaking into the group.

We have had hundreds of these meetings. We have included

thousands of employees, from executives to clerks and secretaries. Out of this experience we have developed a number of ideas about the characteristics of a successful meeting. This list is not inclusive or complete.

First, the key people present (and perhaps the rest of the participants as well) must recognize and understand the problems they have to solve.

Second, they must want to do something about these problems.

Third, they must believe they can accomplish changes or improvements.

Fourth, they have to be in charge of the problem-solving process. They have to supply the information and do the evaluating. No one can come in to administer a solution. An outsider may help, but the participants must feel they are doing the deciding. This is one of the most difficult parts of the whole process.

Fifth, they have to accept their responsibility. The group that says, "If only top management would..." renders itself ineffective. The effective group says instead, "What can we do about that problem?"

Sixth, the group must create an atmosphere that encourages free expression. There must be a chance for airing frustrations and disagreements, including interpersonal ones.

Seventh, they either must have or must develop a determination to achieve changes. It is relatively useless to bring up complaints unless something is going to be done about them. Therefore, the participants must see the extended staff meeting as part of a continuous process. It is not something that just happens every six months. It happens when it's needed, but the real work is done back at the shop: that is where the system works, that is where the environment must be created, where the base for freer expression must be broadened.

And last, but equally important, is the need for the group to identify and deal with the totality of the problem. This is something we learned through experience. In our first meetings we set aside the last 15 minutes of a meeting to talk about process. But if some participant felt either he or his function had been attacked during the first 15 minutes of a meeting he would sit there for the next two hours waiting to express his feelings. Then we tried having a process session at the end of a topic rather than at the end of the meeting; that didn't work very well either. Now we say, "If you have something to say, say it now." We still get the complaints, but we also get people to deal with the totality of the problem, to see the relationships between its technological, organizational, and interpersonal aspects.

In short, our experience has shown that to be effective in these extended meetings and in the team development process, we have to draw on the full range of organizational hunches, hypotheses, and theories. We can't limit ourselves to one man's ideas or one group's ideas. We must focus on working the problem.

## Conclusion

I am not saying that extended meetings are a panacea for organizational ills. I am sure that some of the 175 meetings we will have this year should not be held. I know of some already that shouldn't

*Frank J. Jasinski*

be held. Sometimes they become a fad, the thing to do; the more you have, the better you look. Since the experience can be extremely heady, satisfying, and productive, it can become almost a cult. If it becomes the answer to all problems, it won't succeed. We must explore and experiment to find where it will be successful and useful.

What it seems to me we have learned from these experiences is the necessity for seeking out, for experiencing, for learning, and for exchanging. And this, I think (and I don't know whether I am a theorist or a practitioner), is the beginning of a whole new phase of understanding and dealing with organizational life. Organizational life is not an either-or proposition. The more we can blend the organization and the individual, the nonbehavioral and behavioral approaches, the more effective we can be. In addition, practitioners need to pause and be introspective every once in a while, to look at what is being done, what works and what doesn't work, and why. The theorists need to peek out of their bastions occasionally and talk with the practitioner. Between us, we can probably get somewhere.

**JAMES E. RICHARD**

*Visiting Professor of Management, Boston College, School of Business Administration.* Formerly vice president, human relations, in the Polaroid Corporation, Mr. Richard has had a wide range of experience in industrial positions, including production, sales, and labor relations. He was president of the Red Jack Manufacturing Company, Davenport, Iowa, before joining the Polaroid Corporation.

# INNOVATION AND EXPERIMENTATION
# IN A RAPIDLY GROWING ORGANIZATION

Because I find that I often learn best about principles and theories by examining specific experience, I plan to sketch for you the stages of growth our company has passed through, and the aims that have guided us in our approach to organizational issues, and then to describe a number of the things we have done in our attempt to live out our values.

The Polaroid Company has passed rather rapidly through several stages of growth, having grown to its present size in one generation. The company was founded by Dr. Edwin H. Land when he was of college age, and was then essentially a scientific effort, bent mainly

137

on discovery and invention in the realms of chemistry, physics, and optics. Organization for commercialization came later, and, as the company moved from early stages of invention to the marketing of the first products, an organization of several hundred people was gradually assembled. New products followed, and over a couple of decades the organization grew from hundreds of people to thousands.

From the outset the emphasis was on youth, exploration, invention, long risks. The vision was that achievement comes from continuous simplification, from discernment of essences, and from the courage to try and to fail. The views on human organization were correspondingly lofty and hopeful, and characterized by the same experimental approach that applied to natural and physical sciences. Two fundamental beliefs—in the individual potential for contribution, and in the power of well-knit collaborative effort—formed the basis of organizational philosophy. Superior results were not expected only of the few, for it was believed that there is great power untapped in many people, and that growth is everywhere a potential. The issue was how best to develop and support creative people and a collaborative organization. As the small organization grew, these values were not merely given passing thought; they were actively discussed, clarified, written about, and acted upon.

Thus, as every working organization is a society, the foundation was laid for a culture. The tradition of this new, young, forming company grew from the practice and experience by which its active problems were solved, in a spirit of exploration and discovery.

Two aims were defined, in writing, for the company. One was to make genuinely new and useful products—authentically creative contributions to the world, with excellence the standard. The second aim was to open to each member of the organization avenues for maximum exercise of his talents—not to do things for or to people, but to clear the way for each to make his own discoveries, and for each to enlarge himself and press his competence as far as his will and his endowments could take him. The intention was to keep the organization open, flexible, and responsive to change, and to develop procedures that would permit maximum constructive impact of the individual on the whole.

These values, consciously and seriously held through the ups and downs of growth, were applied in various ways—with experiments tried, discarded, reshaped, and in many cases developed into standard practice.

One of the early experiments, some years ago, was called somewhat romantically "The Pathfinder Project." This was an effort to relieve dull and repetitive jobs, and at the same time to help employees find and develop the most fruitful career paths possible for themselves. The Pathfinder program sought to break up a day's work so that if one part were dull, another part of the day would provide interesting, stimulating work. The general formula was to establish a two-job day for the selected member, four hours on the old job and four hours on a second job, with more challenging, more difficult, more advanced work. There were many problems of implementation, and ultimately the program was abandoned in its original form, but some permanent practices grew out of it.

Another experiment, one that succeeded and survives as an active part of our operation, is now called our job posting system. This system covers all jobs in the company up to officer level. All openings are described in writing and posted on bulletin boards at eighty special job posting stations throughout the company. The name of the requisitioning manager, the department, the job content, and the requirements are listed, and the compensation levels described. Sometimes only the hiring person interviews and decides, but often interviewing teams are used. The name and telephone number of the personnel administrator handling the posted job are listed; he refers applicants for interviews, as appropriate. The personnel officer sees the posting through to completion, which includes seeing that someone follows through with a career discussion with each applicant, the unsuccessful as well as the successful.

There is tremendous power in this system, and we cherish it. The considerable effort required to maintain it is compensated many times over by the benefits to the organization of maintaining openness in the system, providing genuine paths of mobility for members, and building realism and honesty in the career outlooks of both employees and hiring managers.

At the moment, for example, we have a posting on our boards which we call a "general posting." It is as follows:

Since it is not always feasible to post specific job openings at the upper management level, we have in the past used the "general posting" to provide opportunity for people who believe themselves qualified to express interest in such positions.

If you are at or near upper levels of management and want to be considered for additional or different responsibility of this type, interviews will be arranged so that you can discuss your career desires and your qualifications with key managers. This will aid in their consideration of your qualifications for any of the positions which may not be specifically posted, and will provide you with the benefit of their critical advice and counsel. For further information or discussion call (and the telephone extension numbers of personnel representatives are mentioned).

Backing this posting are some teams of officers and key managers who will invest a good bit of time in interviewing. Several of our promising young managers have responded. With the knowledge and support of their own bosses, these young men will talk with several managers on levels higher than theirs in areas of the company where they believe their future interests may someday lead. They will get good, useful, straightforward response that will provide better perspective on their own circumstances and improved knowledge about what is going on in the company. A lot of cross-fertilization will occur, even though immediate job changes may not result.

Another of our practices is career counseling, which has grown out of the old Pathfinder program and out of needs generated by our job posting system. A specialized function of our personnel operation, career counseling is designed to help individuals improve their initiative and personal skill in managing their own careers, to develop a sound capacity to explore and evaluate their circumstances and their environment, and to help them make choices that square their own aspirations with circumstance and opportunity.

Our counseling program and our job posting system have singular sanction and support throughout the company. Although not uni-

141

versally used, they are surprisingly free of management manipulation or distortion, and their integrity is rather jealously guarded by the organization as a whole.

Another activity that we have developed to help keep the organization open and responsive is called career exposure. We've found that one of the problems of organization is that people are often unable to test the reality of situations. To meet that problem, we have worked out a system of job exposure, planned as part of the career counseling process. The idea is to provide real experience to help the employee and his supervisors determine how realistic a change from a present career field might be; recognize the necessary growth required for future success; and determine to what extent the employee possesses necessary interests and abilities, or is likely to be capable of acquiring them. For example, exposure to the actual work may reveal that without additional skills his continued growth in the field of his choice would be restricted, and a plan of further education can be worked out. Of course, he may also surprise himself and everybody else by discovering talents and aptitudes that haven't had a chance before. Again, he may find that although his interest in the new field is certain, personal restrictions (home, family, social activities, etc.) prohibit pursuit of his business goals in that field; he might then decide that to remain in his present field is more realistic.

Here are a couple of examples of typical career exposures that I pulled from the files.

A woman, age 39, had been with the company seven years and was anxious to move from production work. Her children had grown up, and she could begin to see herself as a career woman. She was unfamiliar with other fields of work. Our career guidance department offered her an opportunity to review our career field manual, which describes in detail the range of career opportunities in the company. The career office suggested she watch job postings for kinds of opportunities that appeared most appealing to her. Clerical work had some appeal to her, but typing skills were a prerequisite to growth in that field. After further discussion this woman was placed on an exposure job doing some filing and routine, nontyping clerical work. She discovered that this level of clerical work was not worth the change from production, so she took a typing course. Later she had another exposure job to develop her speed and general knowledge of office routine, and has grown in three years from clerk to secretary.

A 37-year-old man who had been with the company for 13 years had a reputation of being difficult to work with. In earlier years he had moved from stock clerk to group leader but now found himself unable to compete with others for supervisory positions. He had a disgruntled feeling that the company was placing too much emphasis on schooling. Younger, more educated men were coming in, and he was inclined to place the responsibility on others for his lack of growth into supervision. Offered a career exposure to help him determine for himself what he might be able to do without further education, and also to provide an evaluation by another supervisor who would take a new look at his attitude, this man spent three months on an exposure job in expediting. He found the work stimulating and interesting. The supervisor found him personable and able to handle himself well. Later on he applied and was accepted for this job in the normal job bidding procedure. As a result, he rebuilt his reputation and developed an entirely new interest. His present job doesn't require academic competition with others, and he is in a realistic and satisfying career position. These may seem to be prosaic examples, but they demonstrate a corporate attitude toward people and their jobs, the cumulative effect of which is significant; this attitude becomes even more important as the rapidly growing organization takes on age and maturity.

In our education and training programs, we have two avenues of approach which we consider distinct. One features courses in mathematics, physics, photography, reading, writing, and specific management or technical skills. The other is in the realm of interpersonal relationship skills, where our organization development specialists work with groups on problems of conflict, communication barriers, and collaboration. Perhaps our major long-term objective has to do with building increasing competence throughout the organization in handling interpersonal conflict and issues of organization change.

Rather than get into details of how we work at interpersonal relationships to facilitate change, I want to touch upon another general tradition we've evolved to help us deal with organization change. That is a method of developing personnel policies by eliciting the participation of members of the organization. We have a written policy manual that is available to everyone, and we attempt to keep it open to direct influence by the organization membership, through a device we call our "yellow paper" procedure.

Briefly, it works like this: when an issue of operating procedure or of personnel policy arises that affects working conditions, our employees' committee (an elected advisory group that has existed for many years and meets monthly with the personnel policy committee of top management) may research, study, and argue the question and contribute to a proposal by the policy committee. Or the proposal could originate elsewhere—the general manager, a scientist, the personnel group. The proposed new policy or change is drafted on yellow paper, and the yellow draft is distributed throughout the company for comment. On major issues, company-wide discussion meetings may be conducted—perhaps led by members of the personnel department or sometimes by line managers.

Ultimately, often after repeated revisions made in the light of the information and ideas fed back, the yellow paper is converted to "white paper," which means it is given permanent policy status and is placed in our personnel policy manuals to guide our daily operations from that point forward. An example of such a major policy change was our recent conversion from pay by the hour to pay by the week for nonsalaried members of the company. This particular yellow paper went through three major revisions before it became operating policy.

Another important procedure that we have developed is a formal appeal procedure by which an employee can seek redress of a grievance. The procedure requires a written statement of the issue, its history, and the redress sought. The employee can obtain help from the personnel department, the employees' committee, or others. The system requires written responses after hearings at each successive step up the ladder of management. Ultimately, if a complaint is pressed without satisfactory results, it can go to an outside arbitrator as a final step.

We have tried other experiments and innovations in our effort to maintain our company's responsiveness to change and to provide a working climate conducive to self-initiated, self-responsible career growth. I have left it to you to discern the relationships between the examples I have mentioned.

These programs were begun, or the ground work was laid for them, back when the company was young, small, and intimate. The expectation then was that growth would bring more formality, and the desire was to maintain the flexibility, the dynamism, the capacity for boldness, and the potency of youth, despite the advent of size and riches.

Indeed, we have felt the strains of rapid growth. We have experienced the sense of greater distance between people, and between top and bottom; fragmentation of what once had been cohesive groups, working face to face; bureaucratization, threatening individual choice and judgment; and diminished range of contact and influence for practically everyone. As we evolved, new skills were needed, many of which had to come from outside the company, and as new people were brought in, some less educated old timers have felt threatened. During intensive growth periods, some old timers have feared that they were going to be outnumbered, and that other values would come in with the newcomers—attitudes of cynicism, disbelief, impatience. With rapid change and with our posting system, there have been periods when many members of the organization were changing jobs. Old channels of contact and old informal information systems have been cut off, sometimes leaving people with a sense of isolation. I am sure that these are classic experiences in an organization undergoing rapid expansion, and in our case they have been felt to some extent at all levels.

You are all familiar with how apprehension and anxiety, ambiguity and uncertainty about where things stand in periods of change shake some bases of trust. We've found that fear and anxiety are best handled when confronted, recognized, and aired; that involvement builds bonds of organization, isolation alienates people. Our experience has been that human encounter can be a healthy way to deal with organizational stress. Straight information, even when distasteful, can diminish suspicion and fear. It has seemed to us more realistic to be patient with the fact that people often differ and disagree than to try to enforce harmony by manipulation. Reality is how people *do* feel, not how they *ought* to feel.

So we have tried to make the things I have described to you work. And although we have never solved all the problems or found all the answers to all the dilemmas and paradoxes, we are convinced the efforts have been well worth while, and in most cases we believe we are much better off for having tried, even where the result has fallen short of our aim.

## FREDERICK G. LIPPERT

*Director of Employee Relations, American Electric Power Service Corporation,* where, for the past twenty years, he has directed training and management development programs. Dr. Lippert has taught at New York University Graduate School of Business Administration, and is currently an adjunct member of the faculty of the University of Connecticut School of Business Administration. He has been a contributing editor of *Supervision* for the past ten years. His first book, *Accident Prevention Administration,* will soon be followed by *The Participative Leader,* now in preparation.

# PARTICIPATIVE LEADERSHIP

During my many years of involvement in supervisory training and management development, I have become interested in participative leadership and have thought we should learn more about it. But most of the literature on the subject pertains to its effects on the partici-pants—what it does for the people who are permitted to participate. It occurred to me to investigate the other party to the participative process, the leader, the person who lets the others participate. What determines his behavior? What causes him to offer participation to his subordinates—the offer, obviously, on which the entire process depends?

149

*Frederick G. Lippert*

It would seem that most of the experimenters and prescriptors, be they behavioral scientists or organization policy-makers, assume that a manager can readily adopt a participative style of leadership. One author, Miles, who refused to make this assumption, undertook a study to find what value managers placed on participation. He found that most have a dual set of values: when they participated in the decision-making of their superiors, they felt that the human resources of the firm were maximized, but when their subordinates participated, they thought the value lay primarily in the possibility of a boost to human relations or morale. Thus Miles' respondents fancied themselves as valuable participants; but when it was their turn to offer the same opportunity, they thought their subordinates' participation of little substantial value.[1]

This led me to wonder whether managers were giving only lip service to the notion that they should be participative, or whether there were organizational circumstances under which a manager would be moved to make a bonafide offer of participation to his subordinates. I also wondered whether personality differences would affect the readiness of a leader to make such an offer, as Vroom had shown such differences affected the attitude of the participant.[2] Would it not be possible to study both these questions and at the same time to determine what aspects of a leader's behavior convinced a subordinate that he was, in fact, being allowed to participate?

To answer these questions, I undertook two studies. In Study I, the attitudes of 208 members of middle management toward participative leadership were examined by questionnaire. Simultaneously, in Study II, a field experiment was conducted to observe the actual participative behavior of 254 middle managers.

## Study I: The Questionnaire

Each of the 208 subjects was attending one of four middle-management training programs conducted by a midwestern university during the summers of 1965, 1966, and 1967. The average age, organization level, years of experience, etc., of the groups were sufficiently similar to warrant the assumption that a homogeneous sample had been obtained, although admittedly this was a convenient, available sample of the management-professional-technical staffs of the employing organizations, not a true random sample of American middle management.

Each was given a questionnaire, "Problem Solving in Management," which presented two alternative methods for solving a problem or making a decision:

**Method 1.** You might bring together a group of your key people and work out a decision jointly, through group discussion; or

**Method 2.** You might work out the solution on your own and then inform the group of your recommendation.

Each respondent was asked to select the method which he used more often, preference for participative leadership being indicated by choice of method 1.

Each manager who selected method 1 was asked to rank eight conditions under which he might use that method. Each was also asked to rank eight conditions under which he might use method 2, even if he used this method only occasionally.

The authoritarian level of the managers was then tested by admin-

**1.** R. Miles, *Conflicting Elements in Managerial Ideologies* (Berkeley, Institute of Industrial Relations, Reprint 248).

**2.** V. Vroom, *Some Personality Determinants of the Effects of Participation* (Englewood Cliffs: Prentice-Hall, 1960).

istration of a 25-item F scale, developed by Vroom.[3] Since the maximum score was 125, those with scores of 95 or higher were classed as high authoritarians (HF), and those with scores of 60 or lower were classed as low authoritarians (LF). Those whose scores fell between 95 and 60 were classed as medium authoritarians (MF).

Both of the test instruments were included in a packet containing other tests not related to this experiment. The subjects were told that the purpose of the entire test battery was to obtain a measure of their attitudes toward various management concepts. No mention was made of a study or experiment. And, to minimize the tendency to give the desired response, the words "participation," "participative leadership," and "participative management" did not appear.

No significant difference between high- and low-authoritarian managers was found in the self-reported preference for participative leadership. In fact, the percentage of high authoritarians who professed preference for participation exceeded the percentage of low authoritarians who expressed the preference, but the difference was not statistically significant.

Although the HF and LF groups made similar rankings of the conditions under which they would use a participative leadership style, and their rankings for the occasional use of a nonparticipative style were even more consistent, it is interesting to note certain small differences between the two groups. HF managers said they were most often participative "when it would increase [their subordinates'] knowledge and improve their job performance"—they seemed to perceive subordinates as resources that need development. In contrast, more LF managers chose "when I feel my people know more about the problem than I do"—they seemed to see the group as a resource to be employed. The conditions ranked lowest by both groups were "even when I am not sure it is company policy to do so" and "when I work for a boss who asks for my ideas on problems." The subjects were apparently not very worried about asserting their individualism, but, on the other hand, they were not going to imitate the boss.

There were no significant differences between the HF and LF groups in their ranking of job conditions under which they might withhold the offer of participation. Both groups gave precedence to "when I believe it is my responsibility to work out the decision on my own" and "when I believe group discussion will only lead to discord and disagreement." Surprisingly, "even when I am not sure it is company policy to do so" was not cited as important for withholding the offer, nor did either group seem to be influenced negatively by "a boss who makes his own decisions."

Overall, it appears that the subjects' rankings of conditions under which they would select or reject a participative style do not reflect their own levels of authoritarianism. It should be noted, however, that managers are conditioned by teachers, consultants, and literature to respond favorably to any statement advocating participative leadership. In Miles' study only 7 of the 215 managers expressed disagreement with a majority of such statements;[4] in this study, 163 of the 208 managers reported that they preferred to use a participative leadership style.

3. Vroom, *op. cit.* [This F scale, which appears as an appendix, consists of 25 items taken from forms 40 and 45 of the F scale developed by T. Adorno, et al., in *The Authoritarian Personality* (New York: Wiley, 1950)]
4. Miles, *op. cit.*

## Study II: The Experiment

The second study[5] sought to explore whether or not the leaders would behave as they said in Study I, what psychological and situational factors determined whether participation was offered, and how often an offer of participation was perceived as such by subordinates. We also wished to inquire into the possibility of introducing participation by fiat, and into techniques that would-be participative leaders could learn and practice.

We planned to observe the leader under pressure from his immediate superior (the most influential member of his role set), reasoning that in nonexperimental situations the pressure from the superior would reflect the pressures bearing on the superior, and therefore would be representative of the environment. We thought that this pressure from the environment would interact with the leader's own authoritarianism, and that the extent to which one or the other dominated would vary with the intensities of each. Thus, we assumed, an HF leader would comply with clear instructions to be participative, but if he had highly ambiguous instructions he would revert to type and withhold the offer. We expected an LF leader to comply with a clear directive, but to be less likely to refuse to offer participation under ambiguous instructions.

Six field experiments were performed at four locations between June, 1965, and June, 1966. Groups 1 and 2 of Study I formed two of these groups. The remaining four groups were participants in similar management training programs. They had about the same characteristics as groups 1 and 2 in terms of age, organizational status, years of experience, etc.

As in Study I, the authoritarian level of each subject was determined by his score on the 25-item F scale. Those with either high or low F scores were selected as "leaders" and the rest of the group was assigned randomly to the leaders as their "subordinates." Half of the HF and LF leaders received from the program director (the acknowledged "boss" of those attending the program) a statement of a problem pertaining to the operation of the management training program, written so as to be highly ambiguous about the attitude of the program director, the seriousness of the problem, and the need to consult with resource people (i.e., subordinates). The other half of the leaders received an unambiguous statement of the same problem, which made it clear that the program director considered the problem to be serious, that he desired a solution, and that he suggested contact with subordinates.

The problem was placed in each leader's mail box, in a sealed envelope. Three days later, the evening the answer was due, the entire group was assembled and a questionnaire given to each person, by name. Each leader received a questionnaire designed to obtain his report of his behavior while solving the problem, and each subordinate received a questionnaire designed to obtain his report of his leader's behavior. Thus the leaders' and subordinates' responses could be compared.

The results indicated that both the leader's own level of authoritarianism and the degree of ambiguity in the superior's request for participation do affect the leader's propensity to make an offer of participation to his subordinates. Of the HF leaders, all who received a clear directive did offer participation, whereas only eight of the

**5.** Fully documented in the author's doctoral dissertation, "The Participative Leader," New York University, 1967.

15 who received ambiguous communications made similar offers. Of the LF leaders, 11 of the 15 who received clear directives offered participation, and 13 of the 15 who received ambiguous messages did so.

Thus, contrary to the findings of Study I, which were based on self-reported data on participation in the abstract, there is a significant difference in the propensity of high and low authoritarians to make the offer in a real-life, decision-making situation. The most significant finding, in my opinion, is the responsiveness of the high authoritarian to unambiguous pressure. If he perceives that participative behavior is desired, he will be participative. The low authoritarian, on the other hand, appears more prone to participation, but when he is told in an authoritative manner to be participative, he seems to have a tendency to rebel.

The second question we wished to investigate was whether or not there were certain acts a leader could perform which would convince group members that they were participating. The questionnaire listed six carefully chosen acts and asked each group member if his leader had performed them. Each of the 47 leaders who had made some offer of participation was given a numerical score based on the number of these "participative acts" reported by his group; those whose scores were above the arithmetical mean were considered "high participative." The questionnaire also asked each "subordinate" to indicate the degree to which he felt that his ideas influenced the final decision. The numerical values assigned to this level of influence by group members (ranging from 7 "a great deal" to 1 "not at all") were averaged to determine whether the group experienced high or low feelings of participation. Groups reporting an influence level above the average of all the groups were considered high influence groups; groups reporting an influence level below the average were considered low influence groups.

Using these methods we found that of the 47 leaders who made some kind of offer of participation, 25 induced high feelings of participation in their group members and 22 induced low feelings of participation. Three of the 25 leaders who induced high feelings of participation failed to perform enough of the designated acts to be ranked highly participative according to our standards. Two of the 22 leaders who failed to induce high feelings of participation were ranked highly participative according to their performance of the acts. Thus 22 leaders were confirmed as high participative by both measures and 20 were confirmed as low participative. It then remained to correlate the acts of each confirmed leader with his group's self-reported level of influence.

In brief, we found that neither the act of convening a problem-solving or decision-making meeting nor the asking of group members for facts or suggestion is by itself productive of feelings of participation. For example, all of the 22 confirmed high participative leaders asked for facts, but so did 19 of the 20 confirmed low participative leaders. Similarly, all of the 22 confirmed high participative leaders asked for suggestions, but so did 17 of the 20 confirmed low participative leaders.

It is the perception by the group that their facts or suggestions were considered by the leader that is significant. Equally significant are asking the group's opinion of the leader's proposed solution and telling the group what the leader's final decision was. It is these three acts that were, for the most part, performed by the confirmed high participative leaders, and were not, for the most part, performed by the confirmed low participative leaders. Thus, it would seem, these are the acts which produce feelings of participation.

It should be noted that these findings do not rule out the use of group meetings or asking for facts or suggestions. Holding a group meeting is not a barrier to feelings of participation; however, a sense of participation does not depend on or immediately result from interaction taking place in a meeting. Leader contact with subordinates can be productive in a meeting, or with members singly, if the three significant acts are then performed. Similarly, the lack of significance of asking for facts or suggestions can be interpreted to mean that such requests are not significant when they stand alone, although obviously the leader must ask for facts or suggestions before he can perform the significant act of letting the group know that their facts or suggestions have been considered.

**The Need for Training**

The studies indicate that although managers may be favorably disposed to participation, there is a gap between acceptance of the abstract concept and its day-by-day implementation. Lack of attention to the bridging of this gap becomes apparent as one reads the current literature on participative leadership. For example, in discussing the purpose and functioning of a participative management policy, Tannenbaum and Massarik list education of subordinates as one of the "extra-participational conditions for effective participation."[6]

But they make it clear that they refer only to the receivers of the offer of participation, thus implying that the offerers, as a matter of course, have the cognitive and emotional perceptiveness to fulfill their roles effectively.

Studies I and II showed that this is not the case, however. Although 80 percent of those questioned in Study I professed a preference for participative leadership, Study II found that of the 78 percent who attempted a participative style, less than half were successful in convincing their subordinates that they were actually participating.

For the management interested in implementing participative leadership, such findings have particular relevance. They suggest that efforts to introduce this system of management will meet with limited success until a comprehensive training program is undertaken. In addition, as Study II showed, although high authoritarians will readily comply with a clear management directive that espouses participative leadership, low authoritarians must be approached in a more nondirective manner if their acceptance and implementation of participation is to be achieved.

The latter conclusion suggests that, initially, management's interest in this style of management should be transmitted in a low-keyed manner, so that low authoritarians would adopt participative leadership as their own choice. The high authoritarians would not yet receive any strong, direct impetus to adopt participative leadership, but would be made aware of top management's inclination. After an appropriate period of time, sufficient for low authoritarians to introduce participation in the management process, top management could

---

**6.** R. Tannenbaum and F. Massarik, "Particiation by Subordinates in the Managerial Decision-Making Process," in *People and Productivity,* ed., R. Sutermeister (New York: McGraw-Hill, 1963), pp. 458-72.

issue a more clear-cut directive, saying that it not only viewed participative leadership as desirable but recommended it as the management style to be followed throughout the organization.

A vital adjunct to this approach is a program of training focused on developing greater understanding of participative leadership and the practices that make it effective. This training would not only provide the necessary educational foundation but would also reinforce awareness of management's acceptance and support of the participative style of management. Obviously, the development of a specific plan of training to teach effective participative leadership skills will require further study.